FIVE TREATISES
OF THE
PHILOSOPHERS STONE

(annotated)

---

by

Alphonso king of Portugal, John Sawtre,
Florianus Raudorff

- Ancient Grimoires -
Series
(a part of Templum Dianae Media)

Work edited by "Templum Dianae Media."
Illustrations and cover by "Templum Dianae Media"
Layout and formatting by "Templum Dianae Media"
back page and curated introduction by "Templum Dianae Media"

2024 - All Rights Reserved

Before you continue reading, the author and publisher explicitly ask that you read and understand the legal notes to clarify some basic aspects of the relationship between the parties.

Legal note:

this book is subject to exclusive copyright; reading it is intended for personal use only. It should also be noted that it is absolutely not permitted to modify or use any of the sections of this book, either for free or for a fee; it is absolutely not permitted to use, quote or paraphrase any section or sections of this book or its contents without the written and signed consent of the author and/or publisher.

Legal notice about the non-liability of the author and publisher:

The author and publisher affirm and reiterate that all the information contained in this work, taken individually or in its entirety, depending on the sensibilities of the individual reader or reader, may have a didactic-educational purpose or that of mere pastime.

The author and publisher of this volume, while reminding all readers that no warranty of any kind is explicitly or implicitly given, affirm and reiterate that all the information contained in this work, being derived from critical reading of various sources, possesses the highest degree of accuracy, reliability, topicality and completeness in relation to their ability to research, synthesize, process and organize the information.

Readers are aware that the author is in no way obligated to provide any kind of legal, financial, medical, or professional assistance or advice, and indeed recommends that they, before attempting any of the techniques or actions set forth in this book, contact a professional legally licensed to practice, as per current legislation.

By reading this introduction, each reader agrees, explicitly or implicitly, that in no event shall the author and/or publisher be liable for any loss, direct or indirect, resulting from the use of the information contained in this book, including but not limited to errors, omissions, or inaccuracies.

www.templumdianae.co

Ancient Grimoire Series

Ancient Grimoire Series, is a part of publishing Project "Templum Dianae ".

Templum Dianae has been involved in the creation and dissemination of material of philosophical and esoteric interest for more than 10 years, with the aim of helping aspiring initiates, or work brothers to find quality educational material.

For this, the "Ancient Grimoires" rib, is in charge of selecting the best reprints of the past, re-adapting them for new technologies and making them available again for printing to the public, and providing new life and new luster to the great works, and great initiates of the past.

For this reason, the book you are holding in your hands represents not only an important piece of history of our past, but one of the cornerstones of esotericism, which you absolutely must know in order to progress on your path!

**Teaching Materials
included**

Scan this code to get
your Video Course included in the book, an introduction to
the world of the occult and the paranormal

Or follow this link:

https://templumdianae.co/the-witchy-course/

This Material will give you access to Exclusive training materials to improve in your path !

INTRODUCTION

It is with great honor and enthusiasm that Templum Dianae presents this meticulously crafted reprint of "Five Treatises of the Philosophers Stone." This extraordinary compilation, encompassing the alchemical wisdom of Alphonso, King of Portugal; John Sawtre, a revered monk; and the enigmatic Florianus Raudorff, stands as a testament to the rich and diverse tradition of alchemical thought and practice.

The original manuscript, with its beautifully detailed plates and profound philosophical insights, has long been a treasured artifact among scholars and practitioners of alchemy. Our reprint seeks to faithfully reproduce these elements, ensuring that both the text and the intricate illustrations retain their historical authenticity and visual splendor. This edition is not just a book; it is a portal to the past, offering readers an opportunity to engage with the esoteric knowledge and artistic mastery of the original work.

Alchemy, often misunderstood and shrouded in mystery, is an ancient discipline that straddles the boundaries between science, philosophy, and mysticism. Its ultimate goal, the creation of the Philosopher's Stone, symbolizes the transformation of base elements into noble ones, both materially and spiritually. This collection of treatises provides a rare and invaluable glimpse into the varied approaches and interpretations of this enigmatic pursuit.

Alphonso, King of Portugal, known for his intellectual curiosity and dedication to the arts and sciences, contributed two treatises that reflect his unique perspective and deep engagement with alchemical principles. His writings reveal a sovereign's quest for wisdom and transformation, both personal and political.

John Sawtre, a monk whose life was devoted to contemplation and scholarly pursuits, offers a treatise that combines spiritual insight with practical alchemical techniques. His work underscores the intimate connection between inner purification and external transmutation, a theme that resonates throughout alchemical literature.

Florianus Raudorff, a figure shrouded in mystery, presents a treatise rich with allegorical imagery and esoteric symbolism. His contribution is a profound meditation on the alchemical process, inviting readers to explore the depths of both the material and spiritual worlds.

One of the most striking features of this reprint is the inclusion of the original plates from the manuscript. These illustrations are not merely decorative; they are essential to the understanding of the text, serving as visual representations of complex alchemical concepts. Each plate has been carefully reproduced to maintain the detail and clarity of the original artwork, providing readers with an authentic visual experience that complements the written word.

While alchemy may seem like a relic of a bygone era, its principles and symbols continue to resonate in contemporary thought. The quest for transformation, the pursuit of hidden knowledge, and the integration of opposites are themes that remain relevant in modern spiritual and psychological practices. This reprint of "Five Treatises of the Philosophers Stone" invites readers to explore these timeless ideas, offering insights that transcend historical boundaries.

At Templum Dianae, we are dedicated to preserving and sharing the wisdom of the past. This reprint has been produced with the utmost care, using high-quality materials and printing techniques to ensure durability and aesthetic appeal. Our goal is to provide a faithful reproduction that honors the original manuscript, allowing today's readers to experience the beauty and depth of these classic alchemical texts.

As you embark on this journey through "Five Treatises of the Philosophers Stone," we encourage you to approach it with an open mind and a spirit of curiosity. Whether you are a seasoned scholar of alchemy or a newcomer to the field, this work offers a wealth of knowledge and inspiration. Let the words and images guide you through the labyrinthine paths of alchemical wisdom, and may you find in these pages both enlightenment and transformation.

We are delighted to share this timeless treasure with you and hope that it will enrich your understanding and appreciation of the profound legacy of alchemy.

To the Right Honourable, the Earle of Pembroke *and* Montgomery, *&c.*

Right Honourable:

Hough in these last ages Vice hath beene esteemed above Vertue, and men have made it their businesse to advance their fortunes by wicked means; yet if we looke backe to former ages, and the time of *Hermes Trismegistus*, who is said to be *Moses*, and so called from his being hid amongst the Reeds in the waters; and as he was called *Hermes Trismegistus*, he stiles himselfe the thrice great Interpreter, as having three parts of the Philosophy of the whole world (as may appeare in his Smaragdine Table following; out of which all moderne Philosophers grounded their discourses, and bookes:) thus hee might stile himselfe, being allowed familiarity with his Creator. From him likewise we had our first Record for the Creation of the world, and all things there-

The Epistle Dedicatory.

therein: we shall finde, and be satisfied in judgement, that true honour proceeded, and was at first derived from Vertue; and what man yet ever lived, who was accounted or esteemed so Virtuous, Wise, Good, and Rich, as those who had the true knowledge of Naturall Philosophy, and her secret operations, which from age to age, for many ages, was by word of mouth delivered by one to another, wherby many Shepheards, Heardsmen, Husbandmen, and others of like quality (by Gods especiall favour) became great Princes, Governours, and Rulers over the people upon Earth, being thereby enabled to advance themselves to what Riches and treasure they pleased, (as will appeare by the ensuing Treatises,) without robbing or taxing the people of their Countries under their Government in any sort; who also by their Physicall Medicine continued length of dayes, youth, and strength; by which means those old men mentioned in the Old Testament, with many other Philosophers, were not only so long preserved from the Grave, but also thereby wrought many miracles, to the wonder of the world: as well they might, having the power and dispose of the greatest Treasure, and highest Secret that ever Almighty God revealed to mortall man. And being fully satisfied of your Honours most Noble and Ingenious inclination and love to the study of this most Divine and Mysterious Art; which can proceed from no other then a right Noble and Vertuous disposition, and by a Divine instinct: Nor is a man of any other temper fit for the study or knowledge thereof. And considering of a person of Honour, fit for the presentation of these Treatises, well weighing your Honours
inclination,

The Epistle Dedicatory.

inclination, vertuous Disposition, and mature Judgement, holding my selfe obliged to be serviceable to my power, to all faithfull students in this most sacred Art, have fixed upon your Honour, as most worthy of the presentation not only of these my present endeavours, but also of such others as I shall ere long produce concerning either this or any other subject; not desiring Patronage, as is usuall, (considering the Persons by whom these Treatises were first written) but only Your Honours Noble acceptance of so meane a present, from the hand of him that heartily wisheth Your Honour all felicity, both corporall and spirituall, temporall and perpetuall; and in that wish, I rest,

(My Lord)

Your Honours

most faithfull servant,

H. P.

To the Reader.

HErmes, *the Father of Philosophers,(most plainly of any that ever writ) discovered the matter of the Philosophers Stone, but not the manner of compleatment thereof; and as he saith, he came to the knowledge thereof by the mercy and favour of the great Creator of Heaven and Earth, without the direction, instruction, or information of any mortall man, and writ thereof to posterity, fearing damnation if he should not have done the same; since which time many hundred Philosophers have written of the same Science, (which is the highest and greatest secret that ever Almighty God revealed to mortall man;) but so obscurely, that it is impossible for any man to attain to this high and mysterious Art, except he be Piously and Religiously inclined, and resolved to live a serious and private life, free from all other employment or businesse in the world: and such a man without doubt, by the mercy and favour of Almighty God, and with the help of these following Authours, with some others of the best of these latter times, and the* Hieroglyphicks *now cutting and comming forth in Print by the Printer hereof, living in* Little-Brittaine, London, *never heretofore published; which make a full and clear demonstration to the sons of wisedome of the whole worke of the Philosophers Stone, from the beginning to the ending, and giveth a clearer light to the understanding of the Reader, than all the books in the world; so that by the help of these, and such like Books, with the* Hieroglyphicks, *this Art doubtlesse may be attained unto with ten times more ease, and lesse difficulty than otherwise. These*

only

To the Reader.

only I have given thee a taste of, untill the others come forth, which will speedily be effected. And note this, that scarce one of the ancient Philosophers ever writ fully of this noble Science, but whatsoever one leaves out, may be found in another (if you read many of the best Authours.) I have been a Student in this Art many years, and being satisfied of the truth thereof, (having studied many of the best Authours), thought fit for the good and benefit of the faithfull Students of this Art, to cause these to be published, being by some of my best friends thereunto very much urged; and because the Students of this Art should not be deceived by false Philosophers, and worke as they do upon false matters; as Salts, Alomes, Vitriols, Mettals, Minerals, and the like: let them consider the words of Geo: Ripley, an English Monke, who saith: yet the matter of this worke, according to all the antient Philosophers, is one only thing, containing in it selfe all necessaries to the accomplishing of its own perfection.

And *Henricus Cornelius Agrippa* in the second Book of his Occult Philosophy, in the 4. Chap. saith, there is one thing by God created, the subject of all wonderfulnesse, which is in earth, and in heaven; it is actually, animall, vegetable, and minerall, found every where, known by few, by none expressed in his proper name, but covered in numbers, figures, and riddles; without which neither Alchymy, nor naturall Magick, can attaine their perfect end.

And in the *Rosary of the Philosophers*, it is written: but I advise that no man intrude himself into this Science to search, except he know the beginning of true nature, and her government, which being known, he needeth not many things, but one thing; nor doth it require great charges, because the Stone is one, the Medicine one, the Vessell one, the Government one, and the disposition one, &c. And let this suffice, from your faithfull unknowne friend,   H. P.

The Smaragdine Table of *Hermes Trismegistus*, of Alchymy.

The words of the Secrets of Hermes, *which were written in a Smaragdine Table, and found betweene his hands in an obscure Vault, wherein his body lay buried.*

IT is true without leasing, certaine and most true, that which is beneath is like that which is above, and that which is above is like that which is beneath; to worke the Miracles of one thing, and as all things have proceeded from one, by the mediation of one; so all things have sprung from this one thing by adaptation. His Father is the Sun, his Mother is the Moone, the Winde bore it in her belly, the Earth is his Nurse, the Father of all the Telesme of this world is heere; his force and power is perfect, if it be turned into Earth. Thou shalt seperate the Earth from the Fire, the thin from the thick, and that gently with great discretion: It ascendeth from Earth into Heaven, and againe it descendeth into the Earth, and receiveth the power of the Superiours and Inferiours: So shalt thou have the Glory of the whole World, all obscurity therefore shall fly away from thee. This is the mighty power of all power, for it shall overcome every subtle thing, and pierce through every sollid thing, so was the World created. Heere shall be marvellous adaptations, whereof this is the meane; therefore am I called *Hermes Trismegistus*, or the thrice great Interpreter; having three parts of the Philosophy of the whole World: that which I have spoken of the operation of the Sun is finished.

Here endeth the Table of Hermes.

A Treatise written by Alphonso *King of Portugall, concerning the Philosophers Stone.*

Ame brought to my knowledge, that in the Land of Ægypt, there lived a Learned man that foretold things to come: hee judged by the Stars, and the motions of the Heavens, those things which Time was to bring forth which were by him before understood.

A desire of knowledge carried my affection, my pen, my tongue: with great humility I prostrated the height of my Majesty, such power hath passion upon man: With intreaty and my speciall Letters unto him, I sent for him by my Messengers, promising him with a sound affection, great reward both in goods and money.

The wise man answered mee with much curtesie: I know you are a great King, and that neither presents, nor the Law of silver nor gold, nor any thing of great value, but meerly out of affection I will serve you: for I doe not seek that which is too much for mee, and therfore I seeke not after yours, but you.

I sent the best of my Ships, which being arrived

rived at the port of Alexandria, the Doctor Astrologer came aboard, and was brought to mee, curteous with love, for having knowne his great worth by understanding the motions of the Sphears, I alwayes held him in that esteeme and love which is due to a Learned man.

The Stone which is called the Philosophers he could make, he taught it mee, and wee made it together: And afterwards I made it alone, by which meanes my Riches increased much; and seeing that I was able to doe such a thing, and that divers wayes, which alwayes produced the same thing, I will propound unto you the most easie, and therefore the most excellent and principall.

I had a Library of Books of the Workes of Men of many Nations, but I in this businesse did esteeme neither the Caldeans, neither the Arabians, (though a diligent people) nor the Ægyptians, Assyrians, but those of the East, which inhabite the Indies, and the Saracens did my worke, and so well, that they have honoured our Westerne parts.

The present time makes mee to know a sound and true judgement: because thou shouldst give credit or beliefe to it, doe not conceive that I have lied in any point. That which I look after, is not to bury in oblivion the great worth that was in him my Master: but I will not give such an Empire to any man but to him that is Learned.

Now to unriddle this mystery and to propose

truths

truthes in ciphers, though they are obscure, yet by them you may learne, and shall find they are no vaine things; and if thou commest to understand this great Mystery, have it not in thy ordinary conversation, but leave it in the same cipher of this impression, if thou understandest how to explaine it.

This Matter by wise men is called by divers names: and this matter which to the unwise seemes to bee something, to them is nothing, and its nature being equally moist and dry that it will not give one without another; which is a singular thing to have two such different natures meet together in one. The drie is there in a supreame degree, the moist likewise calls for a supream Authority: the hot and cold fight there together, and are contayned there likewise in a supreame degree; and from that equality, comes the name of each of these severally according to the quality: and though the moist be joyned with the dry, yet each of them retaines its owne name.

Our *Hermes* tells us that it is Heaven and Earth, but others call it Man and Wife, and out of their mariage they make other Riddles, which serve for a light to the infirme Globe, and from thence are called by some, Water or Earth, others the cold which is inclosed in heat, so much the wise may understand.

The ancient Chaos, according to my judgement, was knit together by the fowre Elements: This composition is the like, when the division comes to bee made, the Heaven and the Earth comes to bee a fift Essence of all, for this matter is of that kinde, that it composeth all things. In this matter are found united the four Elements in equall parts, so that if one walk or move, the others doe the like, for by one the others are conducted, so much are they equall in their duties one to another, and where can you hope to find a better thing amongst all Animals, then that which is so much approved by all wise men?

Take the Learned Philosophers Mercury, and let it bee purged from its malignancy and foule quality, for it cannot be too cleane; and see that the weight be equall with twelve ounces of the sayd composition, and then put it into a glasse bottle, for no mettall else is fit for it. And the forme of the glasse must be of the forme of the Sphere, with a long neck, and no thicker then can bee grasped with a large hand, and the length of the necke not above a span, and no wider then the Ægyptian seale may cover its mouth. This you must put into an earthen pot, surrounded about with hot ashes, and bee sure with a carefull hand to stop up the bottle. And then you must have an artificiall Furnace made of Clay, so broad and round as that you may fadome at the thickest place. You must not put the pot in the bottome of the Furnace; but hang it or set it in the middle, upon two irons, which must lie Diameter wise, or acrosse, and the earthen pot must stand upon the very centre and crosse of the two irons, that the fire may come alike to it in all parts, and then with coales make a soft fire, but let not your patience bee troubled to keepe it alwayes alike. The fire must not come within a foot of the pot, and the furnace luted up close about the pot, that so the soft fire may keepe it alwayes working, and bee not troubled to keepe the fire still alike, for if it bee the same at last as at first, thou hast done the worke of an able man.

Two

Two changes the Moone muſt paſſe by thoſe Animals, which maketh a month, or the Sun that degree which is called Sextile, without raine; for the worke requires drought: and then you ſhall ſee a paterne of the worke, of which you muſt bee very carefull for unmarrying of it from his firſt matter which is all one. That which time works helped by the Sun and other influences, when taking leave of the Earth, and having drawne out the moiſtnes that runnes in its veins, it is ſo pleaſed with it, that it converts into ſulphur that part which was moyſt before; ſo that all is ſeene as mother Nature placed it.

This is the part of the Earth, Sulphur, Woman, hot and dry; for when it makes its firſt change or trucke, that part is wanting which encompaſſed the humidity; as *Penelope* made warre in the abſence of *Ulyſſes* in Italy, ſo this Widow ſo pale and wan, hopes for the returne of her baniſhed Husband. By equall weights, as firſt with Art mixt with Mercury, very pure, with this mixture you may worke ſecurely in a glaſſe made by the hands of a good Workman, for the firſt and the laſt muſt be one or like; but if poſſibly thou canſt, the firſt venter is the trueſt.

Doe the following Worke in ſuch maner, that you keepe the ſame fire that you did before, which will be ſufficient, and be ſure your fire gives no flame, and be ſure alſo to watch it nights and dayes: and if you take that paine, you ſhall bee ſure to finde an excellent reward. Thou ſhalt ſee the worke in its blackneſſe, and that being changed, as it was firſt borne, which is not yet the thing that mother Nature gave in her firſt degree, but ſhall turne to bee ſo liquid and pure that it
ſhall

shall be like to Inke, so distinct shall bee the forme of this creature from its first being.

Hast thou not seen the Prison which the Silkworm makes for it selfe, where it dies? and out of that carcase dead in the Net it selfe made, in which no corruption can come, but riseth againe in a forme distinct from its first being, then is brought forth and paints it selfe, with wings in a more ugly shape: So our work begins to live with a new spirit, and new substance, from whence must bee continued the perseverance of the body, that so bloud may bee gotten in it. Doe not you then think of making a greater fire, for by that meanes the bloud and body will bee destroyed. Then shall you see the most excellent point of this Divine worke: open the bottle and it will seeme to bee ruined, for there will come from it a very stinking smell. In this degree is certainly the greatest labour of this work: for if it bee continued with the same heat, it wil certainly come to the highest degree of perfection. After this colour is past, you shall see many more different in their likenesse and appearance: the Argos, and the Iris in their splendor, that the following of the liquid humour will cause to bee of divers colours, untill it comes at last to a certaine whitenesse, then augment a little the heat.

Friend, bee not weary of your worke, and let it not trouble your patience, for this is the first point of getting your inheritance. When the Stone is come to the whitenesse, it is then fixt, and can never be disunited, though it should burne 100. yeares, for the union is perfect. Keepe, as I have told you, the fire in one degree, that it may come to such a whitenesse, as to bee
like

like the pureſt ſnow, which is called the ſilver Elixir. But in regard that Gold is more pretious in eſteeme, let it alone in the bottle with the ſame fire, untill the Stone is come from its white into a Citron colour: then increaſe the fire another degree, and thou ſhalt attaine to a pure red. All being rayſed up will ſhew your worke to be ſecure: the body of this being taken up, will be hard and light, and in it you may take notice of the body of *Diaphano*, and the colour of a Rubie, as in my owne hands my ſelfe hath ſeene it; for which the great God is by me prayſed. Then put this into an earthen veſſell, covered with a cover of the ſame, like a diſh, and this ſo well joined or luted together, of the bigneſſe to hold three *begadas*, according to the bigneſſe of the Stone, and put it on a hot fire of flaming wood there to boile. Heere the Stone will calcine in 10. dayes of the Sun, or Sundayes, &c. and being taken out of that pot, it will be an impalpable and Divine powder. The firſt ſubſtance which doth good to all, from whence it hath no quality in his Quinteſſence, but is applied to all, and hath power to do all, and very being of the thing that is applied to. *Ente*, from the beginning of Naturall cauſes: it is neither Gold, nor Silver, nor other Minerall, nor ſubject to the forme of any Vegetable, but hath a diſpoſition to doe good to all. If it be applied to Gold, from it, it takes firmneſſe, as to convert other things into that Mettall. For if to man, by famous workes, it gives him health, what can bee eſteemed more pretious? Under this impalpable Gold, it happens that there is found a bright Earth, but very blacke and gliſtering, which is not the beſt however, for that which is very red,

red, is fixt and stable, though it be mixt with all compositions, and so makes no ingression, but his vertues are very admirable. But with equall weight thou must unite it with its first principall matter, very pure, and joyne or mixe them together very carefully, if you would have it be brought to live: and then, as I told you before, let it come to the moderate beat as at the first, and in the like glasse as I prescribed before, very close shut: and as thou didst with the fire at the first, so must thou doe it now, and in very short time thou shalt see it become blacke, and of the other colours spoken of before, untill it comes to bee red, and will presently turne into a stone. This have I seene done in a short time: and hee that knowes it not, let him know that he walks blindfold.

I have told you the work in plaine words, and how I did it, and saw it wrought, so I did it, and had the reward: and it is no fallacy, seeing that I am a witnesse to it, for which I prayse and blesse God, which gave me sufficient of knowledge, science, riches, honour, and state, which let me never forget.

If thou wouldst have a division of this into 100. parts, and so *ad infinitum*, it must bee done before it hath firmentation or hardnesse, and then your worke will be certaine. Take an earthen vessell covered, and in it put your quicksilver, and when it begins to runne over, drop in your Elixir, otherwise you cannot keep it for running over. Of Gold one part being purged by Aquafortis with foure of quicksilver washt, and foure of what is spoken of before, joyned with great Art, with one of your Elixir, and put it apart in a crooked glasse or retort, and let it feele a fire of coals

ten

ten dayes together, untill they be all mixed together. And if you will make a further progreſſion, put into an earthen pot 100. graines of quickſilver, and put it over a flaming fire, and when the quickſilver begins to ſmoake and flie away in fume, caſt in one part of your Elixir, and then cover it. Then let it coole, and it ſhall prove a very ſoveraigne medicine: 100. parts of quickſilver, according to the fineneſſe of it, this ſhall convert into Gold. But if you deſire to make experience and ſee the operation upon lead, you ſhall there find it as well: neither doth it ſtay there, for its ingreſſion retains that faculty to turne all mettals into Gold: to every thing it is to be applied, and it converts every thing into a well complectioned nature, halfe a graine of this taken into the mouth makes the party ſtrong; the weak and feeble, it makes ſo luſty, that no man was ever more healthy, and time which is pretious to all, brings thoſe that take it, ſound to their Graves.

The beſt of Beſts invites from his ſupreame dwelling place, the moſt unfortunate of all, joyning together two extreames, after which we ſhall ſee him in his greateſt dignity and Majeſty, which now is moſt diſtant from it: ſay nothing till thou ſeeſt the water produce that which is afterward turned into fire; but if thou ſeeſt that play, then hide not what elſe thou knoweſt, for it is worth full eight hundred yeeres; for being come to that paſſe, then thou ſhalt know the worth of it. Then ſhall be accompliſht the fatall time to ſee my treaſure and my ſelfe, and my ſelfe incloſed or containe my ſelfe: I ſhall not be obſcured, and thou ſhalt remaine with my gift that, in this darkneſs thou ſhalt ſee ſuch a light where a world ſhall bee repreſented.

The second Treatise of Alphonso *King of Portugal, concerning the Philosophers Stone.*

He paſt worke of the moſt pure ſtone, is ſo infinite in multiplying, that it is never weary to give, and to give more, ſuch a likeneſſe hath it to its workmanſhip. But if you would know another way to ſeperate the foure Elements, know that this following Treatiſe underſtood, will teach you to do it with more brevity and ſecurity.

Two ounces of gold well refined with one of ſilver, very fine and pure, melted in clay, and this mixture being filed very ſmall, and with purged Mercury ground untill it be well incorporated one into another. Then put ſuch a quantity of common ſalt ſo well mixed, as that the body may be well conglutinated.

Take a glaſſe bottle, ſubtilly to mix theſe, ſo that no unclean thing may come to it (though never ſo little) and then upon a ſmall fire ſo worke it, as that the Mercury may conſume or vaniſh in its own fume. Then you may preſume the Gold will remaine being a body that will endure the fervency of the fire.

Waſh the matter of this mixture in pure fountaine water, ſo that after many waſhings, the water may remaine many times clean, and retaine its ſweetneſſe

concerning the Philosophers Stone.

of taste: then weigh the matter that remains, and if you find it heavier than it was at first, grind it againe with Salt enough, and put it to the fire againe as before.

Thus I tell you, you must doe your worke, and in a very soft fire: and when it comes to bee of its first weight, that which then remaines, will bee a matter spungeous and subtle, and so well disposed and prepared, that you may use it in any Physicke.

And now you must make a preparation with sublimed Mercury, Copperas, and Salt well washt: for our Physick and reall conjunction gives it afterwards his life, grinding it with Salt very small. Then in a glasse Bottle which hath his receiver, put it to make his distillation.

But know that within the receiving glasse you must put water, and place the bottle in a strong furnace, and make a fire of coales under it, and letting it seeth or boyle softly, and it will turn quick, or living, and be much subject to corruption, and with this, worke securely and be not weary.

Nine of these with three of the first composition, joyned and well mixed, and ground together: and all these and the other put into a round glasse, that hath a neck of a span or palme long, and then stop the mouth very close, for which purpose the mouth must not be made wide but narrow.

Thus I tell you the glasse must be, and of a bignesse to hold the quantity of three *begadas*, and according to the roundnesse of it, so have a place fitted to put it in the fire, that there the matter may be well joyned or masht together, then will the tincture be made.

Forty *begadas*, then shalt thou see the East adorned with the beames of the sunne, when this worke shall be accomplished according to desire, to change the present glasse into another, which serves for the receiver of a Still, which being close luted with *lutum sapientiæ*, on hot water, which it must not touch.

The Fire must not bee of any great heat but moderate, that it may worke its effect, distilling its water in a perfect manner, and then doe the same worke over againe ; joine the matter with great wisedome, with this his distilled Water, joine Mercury, of an equall weight with the first matter.

Note my words which I will tell thee, that now thou shalt come to putrifie it, and after forty dayes put it into the Still, keeping the same order as before, for the glasse and the fire, take this distilled water, and in the place where it falls, put in an equall weight of the first matter as aforesayd.

Doe this worke as at the first, for it must be thrice reiterated from time to time, receiving the water that the fire will give to the very last. Think not the time light, and though you passe the forty dayes and more, yet still keepe the water in a glasse bottle.

Change it from the receiving glasse into another, and put it upon hot ashes, and then thou shalt have, or draw out a lighter element in weight, called Ayre, which you must subtily put into a bottle, and stop the mouth of it very close with *Hermes* his seale, and its necke also ; be carefull that you let not forth the aire.

Put in or to the glasse another receiver after, (having strongly luted it) and make such a fire as that by his great heat the pot may distill ; this Element keep
with

concerning the Philosophers Stone.

with carefulnesse, for it is the Element of Fire, and then, thankes be to God, in this worke thou hast separated the foure Elements.

After the division of this Chaos, thou must now thinke of joyning them together againe: for if thou meanest to joyne and make that world which was disunited, the only matter which is in the bottome of the glasse must bee retayned or kept and softned by grinding, and then the composition put into a glasse.

Let this glasse bee round bodied, and long neckt; which glasse or bottle you must fortifie by luting, and set it upon the coales, that it may have the force of the fire, in such a maner that it may rise ten degrees *Titans* Wife of the beloved Bed; and in this maner it wilbe converted into a hard substance.

In another like glasse put this with a quarter of its weight of the reserved water, and then stop the mouth of it well, and put it in a brasse furnace or vessell, and put it upon hot ashes, and keepe such a fire to it, as the matter may become dry as it was before.

This being done, and the congealing and drying being past, as I have said, do the like again, with its fourth or quarter part of that Royall water. The infusion must be reitterated, and the fourth time ended of doing the same work, know that thou hast satisfied the drougth, or drouth, or thirst that this substance had after that water.

Hast thou not seen the earth when it wants raine, how barren it shews? no fruit to be seen, but all looks like a fallow ground; and every thing like to perish. But if the rain falls to refresh it, it makes it fruitfull for generation, or increase, and every seed that is sown

C 3

in its proper time brings forth its fruit.

And continuing disperseth its watery power into all plants and trees, and makes the fruit appeare on every bough: even so goes this matter preparing; the Ayre which you kept in the bottle, you must give drink to five severall times, the tenth part of its quantity at a time, so that in all it must have halfe its own weight, and alwayes at every time be dryed up.

Then on a Copper plate in a flaming fire try this matter, if it will consume in smoake; for you must presume it to be of the nature of the Ganimedes to flie up to Heaven, but if it flies not upwards, then it is not yet well done, but you must give it more water, and trye again whether or no it hath his true spirit.

Cause it to drink a quarter part of its weight that first it was of, which will be the tenth part of the Aire, and as you did it before, so do it again: then prove it upon the Copper Plate, to trye if it will evaporate and smoake: then turne againe to what you did before.

Then put the matter in sublimation, and when you shall see it all rise up: that which riseth not, but remaineth in the bottome, give it drink again according as is aforesayd: prove it again upon the plate, and so continually trye it till it riseth; and then you shall be sure that in the bottome will remain a black earth like a dead body in the glasse.

As the Ganimedes went up to Heaven, so thou shalt see this matter exalted. It shall be demanded from the God of the earth, by *Jove*, from whom it was stolen, it having been left with *Demogorgon*, and shall be restored, and if thou sublimate it, oftentimes

grinding

grinding it untill it come at last to be firme, it will all remain in the bottome of the glasse.

To this matter there wants ingression, because there wants the fourth Element, therefore make this operation in a fire neither great nor little, but when thou puttest it in its inflammation take the pot, and be sure that not one drop or tittle of any foule thing comes to it before thou seest infusion.

If then thou seest it become like wax that it will rope, then thou hast a vast great Treasure, that thy estate shall be advanced to more than the riches of *Midas*. 100. parts of Mercury put on the fire, and when it begins to fume away, then temper it with one of this matter, and presume thou hast brought it to the perfect medicine.

And if another time thou dost the same worke, one part of this applyed to 100 will turn likewise to the second medicine, and one part of this is a great reward, being applied to 100 parts of Mercury hot, or any other mettal being melted, making it becom Gold most high and sublime: For which the Lord be praised.

FINIS.

The Booke of John Sawtre a Monke, concerning the Philosophers Stone.

ALL things consisting of Naturall bodies, aswell perfect as unperfect, in the beginning of Creation were compounded and made of foure natures, and those foure natures bee the foure Elements, *viz.* Fire, Aire, Water, and Earth, the which God omnipotent did congelate, mingle, and married together in his masse of Poyse: for in these foure Elements is the Privity hid of Philosophers; and when their natures be comming and reducted together into one, then they bee made another thing: whereupon it appeareth that all things universall and variable bee of the foure Elements, ingendred naturally and changed together: whereupon *Rasis* sayth, Simple generation and naturall permutation is the operation of the Elements, but it is necessary that Elements be of one kinde and not divers: for otherwise they have not action and passion together: for as *Aristotle* sayth, There is no true generation, but of such as be convenient and agreeing amongst themselves. Therefore doe not search that thing of nature, that is not of nature, or things not according to their nature; for the Elder tree doeth not bring forth Peares, nor the Thorne tree Pomegranats,

D for

for we doe never gather grapes of Thornes, or figges of Thistles; for they offer no things but such as are like themselves; nor doe they bring forth other fruit then their owne. Therefore it is necessary that our medicine bee taken chiefly of such things as it consisteth in; but there bee many men busying themselves and medling greatly and diversly therein, that now a daies goe about to get the same medicine of dry stones, and divers kinds of salts, as of *Sal alkali, Sal. gem. vitriol, Sal-armoniack*, and allome, cicory, tutty, attramentum, saffron, burnt brasse, vitrioll Romane, verdegris, sulphur, auripigmentum, arsnick, and such other unfruitfull matters, whereas neither salts nor alloms, doe goe into, or be compounded in our worke; but the Philosophers named it salts and allomes in stead of the Elements as *Theophrastus* saith. But if thou desire to make the Elixir wisely and perfectly, then learne to know the Minerall Roots, and make of them thy worke: for as *Geber* sayth, thou shalt not finde the terme or end of the thing in the veines of the earth; for sulphur and mercury which be the roots minerall, and naturall principles, that Nature doth make the foundation of her operations once, as in the mineralls and chambers of the Earth, be water, viscous, and a stinking spirit running by the veines and bowells of the Earth, and of them doth spring a fume, which is the mother of all mettalls, joyned by a moist temperate heat, ascending and verberating againe upon his upper Earth, untill that by temperate decoction in the term of 1000. yeares is made a certaine naturall fixation, as more plainly it doth appeare, and so is made mettall, as appeareth in the bookes of *Geber*: Even so of Sol,

(which

(which is our Sulphur reduced into Mercury, by Mercury) is made a water, thicke, and mixed with his proper Earth, by temperate decoction, and from it riseth a fume of the veins of this proper Earth, *viz.* of himselfe, which afterward is changed into a water, most subtle, which is called *Anima, Spiritus, & Tinctura*, that is, the Soule, the Spirit, and Tincture: and when the same water is reduced upon the Earth from whence it came, and sprinkled upon his owne veines, it commeth into a certaine fixation, and is made the Elixir compleat: and so Art doth worke in a short time by the wit of man, more then Nature doth work in 1000. yeares. But yet wee doe not make mettall, but Nature doth make it: we doe not change mettals, but Nature doth change them; but we be Natures helpers or Ministers. Whereupon *Medius* in *Turba Philosophorum*, sayth, That although our Stone being perfectly created in the Earth, doth naturally contayne in himselfe tincture, yet by himselfe, he hath no motion or moving to be Elixir, unlesse thereto hee bee moved by Art. Therefore let us choose the naturall and next mineralls, according to the words of *Aristotle*, for Nature hath procreated all metalique bodies of a fume, Sulphur and Mercury: wherein thou shalt finde no Philosopher disagreeing; therfore it behoveth thee to know the principles of this Art, and the principall Roots thereof; for hee that doth not know the right beginning, shall never finde the right end thereof: for *Geber* sayth in the beginning of his Booke, Hee that knoweth nor our beginning in himselfe, is farre from the attayning or understanding of this Science: for hee hath not the true Root or ground whereon he should

should rayse this Art, or Science, or Worke: also in another place he sayth; It behoveth that our Art be found out by a naturall wit, and a subtile soule, searching forth the naturall principles and true foundations. But although that a man may know his principles, yet neverthelesse he cannot in this follow Nature in all things, as *Geber* testifieth. Sonne, of this Art of Alchymy, we doe open to thee a great secret; Many Artificers in this Art doe greatly erre, which do think to follow Nature in all properties and differences.

Therefore these things thus shortly passed over, as is aforesayd, let us come to that part of the worke artificiall; many men doe write of the Stone, named the Philosophers Stone, but how, or of what it is made, no Philosopher did plainly and openly name; for in these points divers men taught divers things: whereas the truth doth consist in one thing onely; but without doubt and without all errour, we say that this Stone (which is the root of our Art and privity, or hidden secret of God: and whereof many wise men did treat, who did of it make, and did knit many knots, and so deceived many men in making them thereby fooles) is none other thing but man and woman, *Sol & Luna*, hot and cold, Sulphur and Mercury: and heere sticke downe your stake, staying only and leaving to search further for any other stone, or foolishly to consume thy money, and to bring to thy soule heavy thoughts, or sadnesse: for what thou sowest thou shalt reape. And forasmuch as this Stone is divided into two parts, we will speake a little of the first part *Sol*; and note, that without it, our worke cannot be done, as I well prove by authority of learned Philosophers. For *Aristotle*

stotle sayth, of all things in this world, *Sol* is most: and it is the firment of white and red, without which it is not done. Also *Hermes* sayth, There is no true tincture but of our Brasse, that is to say *Sol*: for all *Sol* is brass, but all brasse is not *Sol*: so all *Sol* is Sulphur, but contrary, for in it is nothing of the corruption of Sulphur, but when it is made white in the worke, then it worketh the operation of white Sulphur, congealing and converting Mercury into *Sol*, of the colour named *Obrison* in Latine, therefore use alwayes the nobler member, that is to say *Sol*; for it is the kinde of kindes, and forme of formes; for it is the first and last in mettals, and it is amongst them in their natures, as the Sun is amongst the Stars, but it doth concerne thee to understand well how to choose in what noble member *materiam vel rem homogeneam amborum mundi Luminum*: that is a thing of that kinde which is a kindred to both the lights in the world, that is to say *Sol*: for *Sol* is *homogeneam*, and the spirit hid and covered in that noble member, without which the work is not done. Wherefore *Rasis* sayth, Doe not colour it untill his hid spirit be drawne out, and made all spirituall; and therefore worke thou nothing but that which is very light, and of the most pure *Sol*; which doth illuminate and lighten all lights, and casteth away all darknesse of the night by his power, *viz.* the superfluity of Mercury and other imperfect bodies, when that it is cast upon them; wherefore *Geber* saith in the Chapter of the Quintessence and Projection of the Stone: this Sulpher, lightning and casting forth his beames, and shining abroad of his most cleare substance, doth irradiate and giveth light not only in the

day

day, but also in the darknesse wherupon *Pandulphus in turba Philosophorū,* saith, my Brethren know ye that there is no body more precious or purer than Sol: for as the Rubie hath in it selfe the effect of all precious stones, so Sol hath in it selfe the vertue of all stones and Mettals ductible; for it containeth in it selfe all mettals, and coloureth and quickeneth them, when he is most noble of them and of all bodies, and the head and the best of them: and consider this one poynt more, that Sol is equall in the qualities and parts of it, and it is of a compleat nature of the foure Elements, without any excesse or defect, for by nature it hath part of heat, and part of coldnesse; part of drynesse, and part of humidity; for it is not corrupted, nor corruptible, by the Ayre, nor by the Water, nor by the infection of the Earth, or by the force or violence of the Fire; yet it moysteneth, rectifieth, and adorneth it, because his complexion is temperate, and his nature direct and equall: therefore that Stone is best of all stones, that is most concoct and nearest, or most akin to the fire.

The second part of our Stone is called Mercury, the which is himselfe, and of the Philosophers is called a Stone, and yet is no Stone: Whereupon a certaine wise man, whereas he speaketh of it, saith, this is a Stone, and yet no Stone, without which, nature doth never worke any thing, which both doth, and drinketh up the worke, and of it doth appeare every colour, whose name is Mercury or Argent vive. Whereupon *Racis* saith of it, a worke may be created so, that the same worke may overcome all Natures; it is friendly to all Mettles, and the meane to joyne tinctures, for

in

in it selfe it receiveth that which is of its nature, and doth vomit forth againe that which is strange, or enemy to its nature, for it is an uniforme substance in all his part. Therefore this Stone is named of the Philosophers, Minerall vegitable, and Animall, and also artificiall, it is called Minerall, because it is ingendred in the Mine, and is mother of all Mettles, or else it is called minerall, because that when there is projection made upon it, it is turned into Mettle, and it is called vegitable, for of the juice of three Hearbs mixed together in equall proportions, that they stand in a moist fire forty dayes, there will be growne forth thereof a Stone of the same colour and vertue of the minerall, for the Hearbs be Mercury, Purcelane, called *Portulaca Marina*, which yeeldeth Milke, and Celendine, it is also called animall or vitall, because of himselfe, without any other thing put into it, his Elements being seperate and mixt together in equall weight, and then set in a strong glasse with a little hole to take ayre at in the aforesayd fire, within three moneths there will engender horrible Wormes, whereof every one will slay one another, untill that one onely will remaine, which if the Master feed wisely, it will grow and wax to the bignesse of a Toad, whose forme is terrible, and this Beast is by himselfe Elixir upon Saturne and Jupiter, or it is called animall, because it is made of a thing that hath life, that is to say man: For in old Hedges it is found of the putrifaction of mans dung, and ordinately heated with a subtile Vessell of Glasse, and therefore the Philosophers sayd our Stone is found in every man, and that of the vilest thing, and of a most vile price: Wherefore *Pithagoras* saith, this

Stone

Stone is animall, because it is apt to bring forth Children; also he saith it is cast in Dunghils, and therefore it is vile and rejected in the eyes of the ignorant man. Also in the Booke which is called *Speculum Alchymiæ*, it is sayd, this Stone is cast away in the street, and is found in dunghills, the which containeth in it selfe all the foure Elements, and ruleth them: and this Stone is artificiall, for by mans wit, it is knit together; for certaine men make Mercury of Lead in this maner: they melt Saturne six or seven times, and every time they draw it with Sal armoniacke dissolved; afterwards they take of that Saturne three pounds, and of Vitriol one pound, and of Borax halfe a pound, and then they do mingle altogether, and put it underneath the Philosophers fire, by forty naturall dayes, and then it is made Mercury; and there is no difference betweene it and naturall Mercury, but that it doth not goe into our worke, as naturall Mercury doth.

Know thou the clean from the unclean, for nothing giveth that which it hath not; for the clean is of one essence voyd of alterations: the unclean thing is divers, and of contrary parts, and of a light or easie corruption, therefore put in thy worke no strange thing, nor let any thing goe into our Stone (except such as is sprung from it) neyther in part nor yet in the whole; for if any strange thing be put into it, it will by and by corrupt, nor will that be made thereof which is expected. Therefore purge the yellow body by the adustion of the fire, and then thou shalt finde it purged; and after that thou hast it well purged, beat it most strongly, and utterly, and make it into thin plates, and after beat them into leaves, the thinnest that can bee possible,

concerning the Philosophers Stone.

ble, as Gold-beaters doe, and then so keep them: but the white liquor hath more superfluities, which must of necessity be removed, for they bee *fæculentiæ* of the Earth, which is the impediment of melting, and humidity fugitive, which is the impediment of fixation.

The earthinesse feculentine is taken away thus; put it into a mortar of marble or wood, and adde to it as much common cleane dry salt, and a little vineger, and stirre them strongly about, and rub it very strongly with a pestle of wood wisely, that there doe appear nothing of the liquor, and that all the salt be all black, then wash all the matter with cleane hot water, untill the salt bee resolved into water, and then powre the same foule water away, and then put it to the liquor of salt and vineger, as thou didst before; and doe this oftentimes, untill the liquor bee made as cleane and shining as glasse, or of the colour of Heaven. And last of all put it into a thicke linnen cloth, twice or thrice doubled, and then straine it forth twice or thrice into a thicke vessell of glasse, untill it bee dry; the proportion of the parts is such, for there bee twenty foure houres in a naturall day; to which adde one, and then there be twenty five, this is wisedome: for *Geber* saith in his fourth Booke, and sixth Chapter, Study in thy worke to overcome the quicksilver in thy commixtion. Also *Rasis* sayth, Bodies be of a great perfection; wherefore more quicksilver is necessary: and he saith, that wise men hide nothing but the weight and quantities, and this we may know because none doe agree with other in weight. Therefore there is a great error; for although the medicine be well preparate and

E well

well mingled together, unlesse that there bee quantities, thou hast destroyed all, as to the verity and finall complement, and that shalt thou see in the triall, for when that the body transmuted, bee put into cineration, there it will be consumed late or soone, according as little or much it is changed into equality of the proportions by right, according to reason it will never be corrupted: therefore no man can passe through it, unlesse that hee bee a wise man, that doeth all things according to reason, and true subtilety, and naturall wit.

Euclides being a wise man, counselled us that we should worke but in Sol and Mercury, which joyned together doth make the Philosophers Stone; whereupon *Rasis* saith, white and red do proceed of one Roote, no body of any other kinde comming between or meddling of the kind of Sol; yet it being matter and forme absent, all the effect is deprived, *quoniam ex materia & forma fit generatio vera*; that is to say, very true generation is made of forme and matter, therefore it behooveth thee to know, that no Stone, or precious stone, nor any other thing besides this Stone is convenient, nor yet doth agree to this worke; but thou hadst need to labor about the solution of the yellow body, reducing it to his first matter: wherefore *Rasis* saith, we truly do dissolve Gold, that it may be reduced into his first nature, that is to say, Mercury: and when that they be brused asunder, then they have in themselves tincture abiding: wherefore *Rasis* in the flowers of *Socrates* saith, make the marriage, between the Red husband and the White wife, and thou shalt have the mastery. Also *Merlyn* saith in his Booke:

Can-

Candida si rubeo mulier sic mixta marito
Mox amplectuntur complectaq; concipiuntur
Per se solvuntur, per se quoq; conficiuntur,
Et duo qui fuerant, unum quasi corpore fiunt.

And truly our dissolution is no other thing, but that the body be turned againe into moistnesse, and his quicksilver into his owne nature be removed againe. Therefore unlesse our brasse be broken and crushed asunder, and ruled by himselfe untill it be drawn from his thicknes, and that it be turned into a thin spirit, this labour is in vaine; whereupon it is sayd in the Booke called *Speculum Alchymiæ*, that the first worke of this worke is the body reduced into water; that is to Mercury, and that is that the Philosophers call solution, which is the foundation of all the worke, and it maketh the body of more liquefaction, and of a more hid and privy subtiliation, which said solution by little and little is done by contritions, and light rosting: wherfore *Rasis* saith, the disposition of our Stone is, that it be put into his vessell, and be sod diligently; untill all do ascend and rise up and be dissolved. And it is spoken in *Specula Philosophorum*, that the Philosophers Stone doth arise from a vile thing unto a more precious treasure: that is to be understood, that the sperme of Sol is to be cast into the matrix of Mercury, by bodily copulation or conjunction, and joyning of them together. Also *Pithagoras* saith, that when it is put together with his like, and be mercurified, it is a young tree, bringing forth fruit for the soule; the spirit and the tincture may from thenceforth be drawn out of him by temperate heat: whereupon he saith, you Artificers of Alchymie, know you that their kindes cannot be truly tranfmuted unleffe that it be reduced into his firft matter: Alfo *Geber* faith, all the whole thing may be made only of Mercury, or Lune, for when that Sol is brought into his firft beginning by Mercury, then nature embraceth his owne proper nature, and then there is in it an eafineffe of drawing forth his fubtill fubftance: wherefore *Alfidius* faith, take things of their owne mindes, and exalt them to their Roots and beginnings: Alfo the Booke called *Lumen Luminum* faith, that except that a man do caft the red with the fairneffe away, he can by no meanes come to the Sulphur, Lightning and Ruddineff. Alfo *Rafis* faith in the feventh Chapter, he that knoweth how to turne Sol into Luna, hee knoweth alfo how to turne Sol into Sol: wherefore *Pandulphus* in *Turba Philofophorum* faith, he that hath wifely brought forth the venome out of Sol and his fhaddow, without which no colouring venome is ingendred, and he that goeth about by any manner of wayes to make colouring venome without this, he lofeth his labour, and enjoyeth nothing but forrow for all his hopes.

The Veffell of our Stone is one wherein all the maftery is fulfilled, and it is a Cucurbit or Gourd with a Limbeck round above and beneath, plaine, without any feapolis, not too high, whofe bottome be round after the fafhion of an Egge, or of an urinall, with plaine fides, that it being made thin it may afcend and defcend moft freely and eafily; and let the Veffell be of fuch quantity, that the fourth part thereof may containe all the matter: and note that it is not of any other mettle but Glaffe, cleane, which is a body dy full of light and shining every thing through it, and lacking poores, shewing also the colours in the worke appearing, whereby the spirits passing may successively vanish away; it must also be made right convenient and meet, wisely, that nothing may enter in by it: whereupon *Lucas* saith, let the Vessell be shut strongly with *Lutum sapientiæ*, that nothing may passe forth, nor enter into it, for if his dew should passe forth, or some other strange humour should enter in, all the worke should thereby lose his effect: and although it is sayd by the Philosophers very often, put it into his Vessell and shut it strongly, yet sufficeth but once to put it in and shut it, and in that thou hast fulfilled all the mastery for that, that is more, is done of evill: Whereupon *Rasis* saith, keepe it continually, wisely, shut and set it about with dew, ever taking heed that this dew doe not passe forth into a Fume: also in *Speculum Alchymiæ*, it is sayd, the Philosophers Stone must remaine close shut in his Vessell untill it hath drunke up his humidity, and that it be nourished perfectly with the heate of the fire, till it be made white: Also it is sayd in the Booke called *Beneloquium*, even as there be in a naturall Egge three things (*viz.*) the Shell, the White, the Yolke; even so there be in the Philosophers Stone three things, (*viz.*) the Vessell, the Glasse, for the Egge shell, the white liquor for the White of the Egge, and the yellow body for the Yolke of the Egge; and there becomes a Bird of the yellow and white of the Egge, by a little heate of the Mother, the Egge-shell still remaining whole untill the Chicken doe come forth; even so by every manner of wise in the Philosophers Stone, is made of the yellow body,

E 3 and

and white Liquor by mediation of a temperate heat of the mother the earthly substance *Hermes* bird; the vessell still remaining whole, and never opened untill his full perfection; keep therefore the vessell diligently, and wisely closed with *Lutum sapientiæ Philosophorum*, that the spirit do not passe forth. Also *Rasis* saith, keep the vessels with his tiolls and closures, that thou mayest be able and strong in the keeping of his spirit: also in another place, shut thy vessell diligently, and doe not in any sort make hast, nor cease from thy worke; also take heed that the humiditie do not pass out of the vessell, and thy worke thereby perish; for *Socrates* saith, bruise them in most strong vineger, and seeth it vntill that it be thick, and take heed that thy vineger do not turne into a fume and perish or vanish.

Of the Fires.

THe Philosophers in their Books have chiefly put two fires, a dry, and a moyst; for the dry fire, they call it the common fire, of any manner of thing combustible that will burne: but the moist fire they call the hot, *venter Equinus*, which may be Englished, the Horse belly; but rather it is Horse dung, wherein remaining moystness, there doth remaine heat, and the moystnesse once consumed, it ceaseth to be hot, and this heat doth remain but in a little quantity, or but five or six dayes, but this heat may be kept a longer time, by sprinkling him with urine and salt oftentimes; for of this fire *Pithagoras* saith, the fire of the belly of a Horse hath property not to destroy Oyle, but to augment it, by reason of his humidity, whereas other fires

fires doe destroy it for their heat. Also *Senior* saith, dig up a grave and lay the Wife with her husband in the paunch or belly of a Horse, or rather in Horse dung, untill they be freely with their good wills married and conjoyned together. Also *Alphidanus* saith, hide thy medicine in a moyst horse dung, which is the wise mans fire, for the fire of this dung is hot and moyst, and obscure, having within it humidity, and a holy light, and therefore there is none like to this in all the world, but only the naturall fire of a hot mans body; that is in health, and this is the secret cause of the strife of the Sea, and not fully combust bloud of man, and the bloud of the red wine is our fire; the Regiment of our fires is such, that the medicine to white must be put into the moyst fire, untill the full compliment of whitenesse, and that the heat must be lent and continuall from the beginning, untill the colour of whitenesse appearing in the vessell, for the lent fire is the conservation of humidity; whereupon *Pandolphus* saith, Brethren, know that the body is dissolved with the spirit whereunto it is mixed, by a most lent decoction, and so the body is thereby made spirituall with the spirit: Also *Astavus* saith, the lent fire doth send forth the spirits of life; the excessive fire doth not make equall the Elements, but rather it wasteth the humidity and destroyeth all things: therefore *Rasis* saith in his high worke, take heed in thy sublimation and liquefaction, lest that when you set your fire on fire, the water also do ascend to the top of the vessell, for if it be so, then it being cold it will stick there, and so thou canst not make thy Sulphur, nor open thy Elements, because it is necessary

that

that every one of them in their sphericall, or spirituall motion be very often thrust downe and lift up, for only the temperate fire is inspicive and perfective of mixtion: Therefore *Botulphus* saith, a lent fire which is called a cleare fire, is the greatest cause of true operation in the Elements. Also *Rasis* saith, it is our light fire, as in an Egge that is nourished, untill the body be derived, and the tincture drawne forth, for by light decoction the fire congealeth the water, and draweth forth the humidity of the corruptive part, and the combustion of drinesse is prevented. Also all the benefit of this worke is in the temperatenesse of the fire; therefore alwayes take heed of a greater fire, that thou come not before thy time to solution, for that bringeth to desperation: wherfore *Rasis* saith, take heed of the intention of the fire, for if it be set on fire before the time, then it is made Red before the due time, which doth not profit, and that he may shew thee the time of decoction. He saith, the solution of the body, and the congelation of the spirit must needs be made with light decoction of the fire, and with moyst putrifaction in forty daies. Also heare *Hortulanus* saying, know ye that in mingling them together, it behooveth you to mingle the crude, quick, sincere, and right Elements together upon a soft fire, and to take heed of the intention of the fire, untill the Elements be joyned together. *Bonellus* saith also, by a temperate heat the body is made sweet and convenient.

Be of a constant minde in thy work, and do not labour in or upon divers matters or things, proving sometimes this matter, and sometimes another; for in the multitude or diversity of things thy Art consists

not,

not, nor is finished, for there is but one subject or medicine, one vessell, one regiment, and one disposition thereof, for all the mastery doth begin in one manner of fashion, and endeth in one manner of mantion; yet the Philosophers did put many works and crafts thereof for the honour and hiding, and prolonging of this Art: as to seeth, to mingle together, to rost, to sublime, to grind, to break, or beat assunder, to congeale, to adiquate, or make even in quality, to putrifie, to make white, to make red; of which things yet there is but one Regiment, which is but to decoct onely. Therefore crush it assunder, and seeth still that thou be not weary: also *Rasis* saith, seeth without intermission. Do not hast or cease at any time from thy worke, nor go about to practise or use the sophisticall bounds of thy works, but onely intend to the compliment of this worke: also *Rasis* saith, it is most sure for thee to apply thy worke diligently, nor do thou leave off thy worke, being as it were a tree cut downe from the bowes; be thou therefore stedfast; and of a long continuall minde and will in the Regiment. Shut most close thy vessell; and cease at no time, for there is no generation of things but by a continuall motion, exclusion of ayre, and heat temperate. Study and marke also, when that you are in your worke, all the signes that shall appeare in every decoction, and remember them, for they be necessary for the workman, to the compliment and fulfilling of this worke, for it is necessary to continue the worke, and moderate the fire; therefore all these things disposed as aforesaid, put the vessell with the medicine in the moyst fire so, that halfe the vessell be in the fire and the other halfe without,

without, to this intent, that every day it may be looked upon, and within forty dayes the overpart, or outside of the medicine, shall appear black like Tarr, and that is a signe, that the yellow body is truly turned into Mercury: therefore *Bonellus* faith, where that you do see blackness appeare to that water, know ye that now the body is liquefied: and that truly is the same that *Rasis* faith, the disposition of our Stone is one, that it be put in his vessell, and that it be throughly sodden, untill all do rise, and ascend dissolved. Also in another place, continue upon him a temperate heat, untill that it be dissolved into water impalpable, and that all the tincture do go forth into blackness, which is a signe of solution.

1. Also *Lucas* sayth; When thou seest blacknes inure to that water in all things, then know that the body is liquefied; for the Philosophers doe call this blacknes the first mariage, for that the man is joyned to the woman, and it is a signe of a perfect medicine and mixtion, but all the tincture is not drawne forth all at once, but it goeth forth by little and little every day untill that in a long time it be compleat and finished; and that, that is dissolved doth ever goe up to the topward, although that which is remayning beneath bee the more: whereupon *Avicen* sayth, that, which is spirituall doth ascend up into the Vessell, and that which is thicke and grosse, remayneth in the Vessell beneath: but this blacknes is named by the Philosophers with many and sundry names; as the fire, the soule, the clouds, the crowes head, oyle, tincture, rednesse, or shadow, Sol, brasse, blacklead, black water, sulphur, and by many other names: and that the

blacknes

blacknes doth conjoyne together the spirit to the body: wherefore *Rosarius* sayth, by the continuance of the fire in the Regiment to the number of forty dayes, both shall be made a water permanent, the blacknesse being covered; which sayd blacknesse, if it bee governed as it ought to be, it doth not stay away above forty dayes of the colour of blacknesse. Also *Pythagoras* sayth, as long as the obscure blacknesse doth appeare, the woman doth rule, which is the first strength of our stone; for unlesse that it be black, it cannot be white nor red. Also *Avicen* in the Chapter of Humors saith, heat in moistnesse doth first make blacknesse, and his moistnesse endureth untill the superfluity thereof bee removed, and then it becommeth white. Also in our works, first they be made blacke, secondly white, and thirdly by a greater intention and composition of fire, it behoveth to be made yellow: whereupon it is written in the Booke called *Multifary*, in the sixth Chapter in the first detection, which is called putrifaction when our Stone is made black, that is to say black earth, by the drawing forth of his moistnesse, wherein the whitenesse is hid, and when the same whitenesse is reversed upon his blacknesse, and is fixed with his earth by easie tosting, then is made the white; in which whitenesse the rednesse is hid; and when it is well sodden, by augmentation of the fire the same earth is then turned into rednesse, as after it shall be taught.

Now againe let us returne to our black Stone, being strongly closed in his Vessell, let it stand therefore continually in the moist fire untill that the white colour doe appeare like unto the manner of most white

F 2 Salt,

Salt, and this colour according to the Philosophers, is called Sal Armoniack, without which nothing can be made, or is profitable in our work: And so the intensive whitenes appearing, the perfect mariage & copulation indissoluble of the Stone is made: then is that of *Hermes* fully fulfilled, saying, That which is above, is as that which is beneath is. That which is above is to obtaine Miracles of one thing: But *Pithagoras* saith, when that you do see whitenes comming above, then be you sure that rednesse is hid in that whitenesse; but before that the white doe appeare, many colours shall appeare.

Therefore *Diademes* saith, seeth the man and vapour together, untill that both of them be congelate into drynesse; for unlesse that it be made dry, divers colours will not appeare; for it is ever black, as long as moystnesse doth rule, and then it sendeth forth divers colours; for in divers manners, and at divers times, it will be moved from colour to colour; untill it come to a firme whitenesse: Also *Zenon* saith, all kinde of colours will appeare in it untill the black humidity be dryed up; but of such colours take you no great care for they be no true colours; for it shall very often times be citrine, and very often times rednesse will appeare, and often times it will be dry, and also liquid before whitenesse; but the Spirit will never be fixed with the body, but with white colour. *Astavus* sayth, betweene the blacknesse and the white, there shall appeare all colours, even as many as can be named or thought of: from diversity of which colours, divers men gave it divers names, and almost innumerable names; for some did it on purpose to conceale and obscure the Art, and some did it of envie: but in the

Chapter

Chapter of the appearing of divers colours in the medicine, there is a definition of his blacknes: for wheras the blacknes and the white be extreme colours, and all other colours be meane colours, therefore as often soever as any thing of the blacknes doth descend, so often another colour and another doth appeare, untill it be an extreame whitenesse: But for descending, and ascending *Hermes* saith, it ascends from the Earth up to Heaven, and descends againe from the Heaven to the Earth and receiveth the superiour strength, and the inferiour strength. And note, that if there appeare between the black and the white any yellow colour, care not for them, for they do not continue, nor are permanent, but they are slippery and passing away; for there can be no permanent nor perfect Red, except that go before it. *Rosarius* saith, no man can come from the first to the third, but by the second; for it appeareth that the white is to be looked for in the second, when that it is the compliment of all the worke; for afterwards it will never be varied into any other true permanent colour but Red.

Now we have the white, therefore now it behooveth thee to make Red, for the white medicine and the red do not differ between themselves in any essence, but onely in this poynt, that the red medicine hath need of a greater subtiliation, a longer digestion, and a hotter fire in his Regiment: And therefore forasmuch as the end of the operation of the white is the beginning of the operation of the Red: and forasmuch as that which is the compliment of the one, is the beginning of the other: therefore unless that thou do first make white the medicine, thou canst never make true red. But now how it shall be made Red, we will tell thee shortly. First the medicine to the Red must be put into our moyst fire, untill the white colour appeare, as is aforesaid: afterwards, let the vessell be drawn out of the fire and put it in a pot of sifted ashes, and warme water halfe full, and let your vessell of glasse with the medicine in the ashes unto the midst, and under the earthen pot make a dry temperate fire and continuall, but the heat of this dry fire must be greater by double at the least, than was the heat of the moyst fire, and by the benefit of this fire the white medicine shall receive Red tincture; truly thou canst not erre if thou wilt continue the drye fire: whereupon *Rosarius* saith, with a dry fire, and a dry calcination rost the dry untill that it be made like Cynaber. Whereto from thenceforth put nothing, neither Oyle, or vineger, or any thing whatsoever it be, untill it be rosted to a compliment of Rednes; and of a truth, the more Redder that the medicine is made, the more stronger it is, and of more power, and that is more rosted will be more Redder, and that which is most rosted is most precious, therefore with a dry fire, burne it without feare, untill that it be closed most redly: whereupon a Philosopher saith, in continuing the Red, seeth the white untill that it be cloathed in purple, and beauty; but some have it; continue the Red and the white untill it be cloathed in purple cloathing: do not cease, although the Red do a little slack to appeare, for the fire being augmented, as I sayd before, after white of the first colours appeareth a mean Red when among these colours shall appeare a yellow, but his colour is not continuing, for after that

concerning the Philosophers Stone.

that it be perfect, Red will not much tarry to appeare, which appearing, be thou certaine that thy worke is perfect: for *Hermes* saith, in *Turba Philosophorum*, between white colour and Red, there appeareth only but one colour, *viz.* Citrine, which is yellow, but it varieth more or lesse: also *Maria* saith, when thou hast true white, thou then afterwards shalt have a false yellow, and afterwards a perfect Red: And then thou shalt have the glory of the clearenesse of all the World.

The first manner of Multiplication of our Medicine.

ELixir is multiplyed by two manner of wayes; that is to say, by solution of heat, and by solution of drying: by solution of heat is thus. Take the medicine and put it into the vessell of glasse, and bury it in our moyst fire seven dayes or more, untill that the Medicine be dissolved into water without any troublousnesse appearing in it. But the solution of drying is that that shall take the vessell of glasse with the medicine, and hang it in a brass pot (having a straight mouth) in boyling, and let the mouth be close, that by the vapour of the boyling vapour ascending, the medicine may be dissolved. And note, that the same boyling water must not touch the vessell of glasse with the medicine, by the space of three fingers: and this solution is made strongly in one day, or two, or three. After that the medicine is made and dissolved; take it from the fire to coole, to fix, to congeale, to harden or dry, and so let it bee very often dissolved; for the

oftner

oftner it be resolved, so much the more perfect it is; whereupon *Bonellus* saith, when that our brasse is turned, and very oftentimes reitterate, it is made better then it was before, and such a solution is a subtiliation of the medicine, and his vertuous sublimation; whereupon the oftner it is sublimate or subtiliated, so much oftner it getteth a greater Virtue, and a greater tincture, and coloureth more abundantly, and the more it shall make perfect and convert, and turne the more; whereupon in the fourth solution it shall get so much virtue and tincture, that one part shall be able upon 1000. of Mercury cleansed, that it shall convert it into Gold or Silver, better then that which is taken out of the Mines of the Earth: Whereupon *Rasis* saith, the multiplication of this goodnesse dependeth wholely on the often reitteration of the sublimations, and fixation of the perfect medicine, for the oftner that the order of this compliment be reitterated, so much more doth increase the nourishment thereof, and the vertue and strength thereof is augmented: for the oftner then was wont that thou shalt sublimate and dissolve the perfect medicine, so much the more oftner thou shalt win and gaine at every time to cast one upon 1000. as if at first it fall upon 1000. the second time it will convert 10000. the third time it will be cast upon, and convert 100000. and the fourth time upon 1000000. the fift time upon an infinite: For *Merodus* saith, know ye for certainty, that how much the more and oftner our Stone is dissolved, so much the more is the spirit and body conjoyned together, and of this for every time the tincture is multiplyed.

The second way of multiplication is another way; the

the medicine is multiplyed by fermentation, for the ferment to white is pure Silver, and the firment to red is pure Gold: therefore caſt one part of the medicine upon ten parts, or twenty of the firment, and all ſuch ſhall be medicine; and put it upon the fire in a Veſſell of Glaſſe, and ſhut it well, ſo that no ayre may enter nor paſſe forth, and let it be diſſolved or ſublimated ſo often as thou wilt; and as thou doeſt the firſt medicine, and one part of the ſecond medicine ſhall receive as much as one part of the firſt medicine. Whereupon *Raſis* ſaith, now have we fully made our medicine, hot and cold, dry and moiſt, equally temperate; whereof whatſoever we doe put to it ſhall be of the ſame complexion that it is put to; therefore conjoyne or marry him that he may bring forth fruit like unto himſelfe: But yet doe not conjoyne or marry it with any other thing to convert it, but with it that it was in the beginning; whereupon it is written in *Speculum*, this ſpirituall earth which is the Elixir, muſt be firſt in his owne body, from whence it was taken at the beginning of his ſolution, that is to marry his earth, and it being ſo rectified and purified by his ſoule to conjoyne it by conjunction of his body, from whence it had its beginning; alſo it is ſayd in the Booke called *Gemma ſalutaris*, the white Worke hath need of a white firmentation; whereby when he is white with his white firmentation, and when he is made red in his red firment; for then that white earth is firment of firment; for when it is joyned to Luna, all is firment to caſt upon Mercury, and upon every body being unperfect mettle to make it Luna: And with the red thereof muſt be joyned Sol; and
that

that is medicine upon Mercury, and Luna to make it Sol. Also *Rafis* saith, it behooveth that he be mingled with wite and red quickſilver of his kinde, and that it be contained and kept that it fly not away; wherefore we bid that quickſilver be mingled with quickſilver, untill that one cleare water be made of two quickſilvers, and not to make three mixtures untill every one of them be diſſolved into water; but in their conjunction put a little of the Worke upon much of the body, as upon foure, and in a certaine time it will be made in the nature of powder, which is of red or white colour, and this powder is Elixir compleate. And truely the Elixir muſt be of a ſimple powder; alſo *Egidius* ſaith to 25. Stones of ſolution, put ſolution, and to ſolution deſiccation, and put all to the fire, and keepe the fume, and take heed that nothing flye from it, tarry and dwell nigh the Veſſell, and behold and obſerve the marvellous working, how it ſhall be removed from colour to colour in leſſe then an houre of a day, untill that it commeth to the marke or prick, or butt of whiteneſſe or redneſſe, for it will ſoone melt in the fire, and come all into the Ayre; for when the fume doth fill the fire, it will enter into the body, and the ſpirit will then be pulled together, and the body will then be fixed, cleare white or red: Then divide the fire, ſuffering it to coole, and be cold: For and if one of theſe doe fall upon 1000° or Mercury, or any other body, it turneth it into the beſt Gold or Silver, according as his firment is prepared; wherefore it doth appeare, that he who doth not congeale quickſilver that will ſuffer the fire, and joyne it to pure Silver, he deſireth no right way to the white worke; and

he

concerning the Philosophers Stone.

he who doth not make a red quickſilver that can ſuſtaine all fire, and joyn it to meer gold, he taketh not the right way to the Red worke, for by ſolution and fermentation the worke or medicine may be multiplyed into an infinite: and note that the Elixir giveth a very light fuſion or melting even like wax: whereupon *Roſarius* ſaith, our medicine neceſſarily ought to be of a moſt ſubtile ſubſtance and pure adherence, cleaving to Mercury of his nature, and of a moſt thin, and eaſie liquefaction as water; alſo in the booke which is named *Omne datum optimum*, when the Elixir is well prepared, it ought to be melted upon a burning plate, or upon a burning cole, even as wax melteth, for that thou doſt in the white, doe it in the red, for the ſame is the operation of both, as well in the multiplication, as in the projection. *Geber* the Philoſopher doth beare witneſſe in his fift Booke, and tenth Chapter, that there be three Orders of Medicines; of the firſt Order is that which is caſt upon imperfect bodies, and doth not take away the corruption, but imperfection, for it doth give tincture, but that tincture doth go away in examination.

The medicine of the ſecond Order, is that which is caſt upon imperfect bodies, and doth give tincture to them in examination; for after the examination the tincture doth remaine, but all the corruption of the bodies is not cleare taken away for ever by that medicine.

In the third Order, the medicine is that which is caſt upon imperfect bodies, and taketh away all their imperfection and corruption, and from corrupt Mineralls it bringeth them into incorruptible. But the

G 2 two

two first of these medicines being left off, we will speake something of the projection of this medicine of the third degree.

The perfect medicine truly is cast 1000, or upon more, according as the medicine is prepared or advanced by dissolution, sublimation, and subtilliation; but because so little, that is, so little is cast upon so little, by reason of the littlenes thereof, it should not be lift up before his virtue be fulfilled. Therefore the Philosophers made their projection diversly, wherefore this is the best way.

Let one part be cast upon a hundred of Mercury, and all is medicine, and it is called the second medicine; and let every one part of this second medicine be cast upon a hundred of Mercury, and all is medicine, and is called the third medicine, and is made 1000. yet againe, let every part of this third medicine be cast upon 1000. of mercury, and it shall be medicine, and all shall be the best Luna or Sol. And note that the third and the second may be so much dissolved, and subtilliate, that it shall receive a greater vertue, and that it may be multiplyed in an infinite: after receive and make projection; first multiply 10. into 10. and it will make 100. and 100. by 10. multiplyed will be 1000. &c.

But how the projection ought to be made, shall be now taught. Put the body upon the fire in a Crucible; also if it be a spirit tepescat, let it do like luke-warme water, and cast the Elixir into it, as is aforesaid, moving it well, and very soone when the Elixir is liquefied, and hath mingled it selfe with the body, or with the spirit, remove it from the fire, and thou shalt have

by

by the grace of God, gold, and silver, according as the Elixir is prepared.

In short therefore, it appeareth by the premisses, that our worke doth consist in the body of Magnesia finished; that is, of Sulphur, the which is called Sulphur of Sulphur, and Mercury, which is called Mercury of Mercury: Therefore as it is aforesayd, with one thing, that is our Stone, with one part, that is to say seething, and one disposition, that is to say, first, making of it blacke; secondly, with making of it white; thirdly, with making of it red; and fourthly, with making of projection, all the whole mastery is finished.

Of the other part of the false Alchymists, and they who doe beleeve them by their distillations, sublimations, calcinations, conjunctions, seperations, congelations, preparations, dissolutions, manuall contritions, and other deceptions, saying, that it is by a similitude onely called an Egge, and teaching another sulphur from ours, and another Mercury from ours, and that it may be drawne from some other thing, or effected by some other then our light fire.

These be all either deceivers, or mightily abused.

For by what and how many soever names it bee called, it is but one and the same thing. Also *Lucas* sayth, Doe not thou passe or regard for plurality of compositions in nature, which the Philosophers diversly set downe in their Bookes; for certainly there is but one thing in all the World, wherein the spirit
we

we seeke for is to be found of any profitable and comfortable use, with which every body is coloured; for in the Philosophers diversity of names, and compositions, they but cover and hide their Science.

FINIS.

A Treatise of Florianus Raudorff, *of the* Stone, *or* Mercury *of the* Philosophers.

In the name of the Father, Son, and Holy Ghost.

A short Declaration of the Great Matter.

CHAP. 1.

KNow yee, that our Medicine is made of 3. things, *viz.* of a body, soule, and spirit. There are 2. bodies, *viz. Luna* and *Sol*. *Sol* is a tincture, wherewith imperfect bodies are tinged into *Sol*, and *Luna* tingeth *Luna*: for Nature produceth or bringeth forth only its like: as a man a man, a horse begets a horse, &c.

Proved by Examples.

We told and named it with names, namely the bodies that serve to our worke, which of some are called Ferment: for as a little leaven leaveneth the whole masse, so *Luna* and *Sol* turne Mercury as their meale, into their nature and vertue.

CHAP. 2.

YOU may say, if *Luna* and *Sol* have a prefixed tincture, why doe they not tinge imperfect mettals? Answer: A babe though borne a man, doth not mans actions: it must first bee nourisht and bred to an age: so it is with mettalls also; they cannot shew their operation,

peration, unlesse they be first reduced from their grosnes to a spiritualty, nourisht and fed in their tinctures, through heat and moistnesse. For the spirit is of the same matter and nature with our medicine; for wee say, our medicine is of fire, Nature, and much subtiler, but of themselves they cannot bee subtile nor simple, for they must bee helped with subtile penetrating things.

Note, earth of it selfe may not be subtile, but must be made subtile, through moyst water, which is dissolving, and maketh an ingresse for *Sol*, that shee may penetrate the earth, and with her heat she maketh the earth subtile, and in that way the earth must be made subtile, so long till it bee as subtill as a spirit, which then is the Mercury, more dissolving then common water, to dissolve the sayd mettalls, and that through the heat of fire, to penetrate and subtiliate the mettalls.

CHAP. 3.

IF you aske, why is Mercury called a better spirit then others, as there are sulphur, orpiment, arsenici, salarmenic, all these are called spirits also: for being set into the fire, they are carried away, and wee know not what is become of them; but this Mercury is much subtiler and clearer or penetrative, then the other; and mettalls are turned in it, but the others burn them, and destroy them, make mettalls more grosser then they were.

CHAP. 4.

BUT Mercury is of such a subtile nature, that he turnes mettalls into simples, as himselfe is, and draweth them unto him.

Note

concerning the Philosophers Stone.

Note, no mettall may be turned by any of the other foure spirits, for if you put any of them to our mettle, it turneth to ashes or earth; but if you doe it to Mercury, it will bee impalpable, therefore is it called argent vive.

CHAP. 5.

WE take nothing else to subtilize mettles; or make them penetrative, nor to tinge other mettles; some call it argent vive, or a water, an acetum, a poyson, because it destroyeth imperfect bodies, and divideth into severall members and formes, as you shall heare, and is called by severall names.

CHAP. 6.

YOU may say, we doe not speake true, that our medicine is made of two things, of body and of spirit; it is right sayd, that all mettals have one root and originall.

CHAP. 7.

WHY can it not be made of two compounded together? Answer, 1. They may be made of all these together. 2. They must be reduced into a Mercury, which would fall difficult by reason of mans life; therefore we take the next matter, which are the two above sayd things; *viz.* the body and spirit: Some Philosophers say in their Bookes, our medicine is made out of foure things, and it is so, for in mettles and their spirits are the foure Elements; and others say true also, saying, mettalls must be turned into argent vive: Heerein many learned and wise men doe erre, and lose themselves in this path.

H *Chap.* 8.

CHAP. 8.

Having spoken of the matter, of which our medicine is made or joyned, or generated; now we will speake of the forme of the Vessells, in which it is made.

CHAP. 9.

Forme of the Vessell.

It is requisite that the Vessell be likened to the firmament, which encloseth and encompasseth all. For our medicine is nothing else but a change of Elements one into another, which is done by the motion of the firmament; and so it must needs be round and circular.

CHAP. 10.

We must speake also of the other or second Vessell, and that also must be round; and must be lesse then the outward Vessell; two hand-breadth high, called Cucurbite containing; on the Cucurbite you set an Alimbeck, through which the vapours ascend to the nose of the Alimbeck; which must be well luted: The Lute is made with meale, sifted ashes, white of an Egge, &c. or one part of meale, one part of calx vive, tempered with the white of Egges, which you must lute withall quickly; lute it well, that no spirits may get away; which if you lose any of them, will prejudice your Worke mainely; therefore be cautious.

Chap. 11.

CHAP. 11.

Forme of the Oven.

THis Oven muſt be round foure hands high, and two broad, and one in thickneſſe, to keepe in the heate the better. Having ſpoken of the forme of the Veſſell and Oven: now we will declare how our medicine is generated and nouriſhed.

CHAP. 12.

How the matter is extracted, and cheriſhed.

WEE ſay that our matter is generated through the heat of fire, and through the vapour of the water, and alſo of Mercury, and is nouriſhed in this manner: and to bring this matter into a juſt compariſon, it is requiſite to prick up your eares, and to open your reaſon and underſtanding, that we may the better underſtand the following Chapters.

CHAP. 13.

First we will ſhew the order of the worke in the following Chapters.
1. The firſt is called Diſſolution. 2. Separation. 3. Sublimation. 4. Fixation, or Congelation. 5. Calcination. 6. Ingreſſion.

CHAP.

CHAP. 14.

What is Dissolution?

IS the turning of a dry thing into a wet one; and you must know, that dissolution belongeth onely unto bodies, as to *Sol* and *Luna*, which serve for our Art: for a spirit needs not to be dissolved, being a liquid thing of it selfe, but mettalls are grosse and dry, and of a grosse nature; therefore they must be made more subtile; the reasons why they must be subtillized.

CHAP. 15.

THe first is, our medicine must needs be subtile, and mettalls cannot bee made subtile unlesse through dissolution, being reduced into a water, and ascend through the Alimbeck, to be turned to water and spirit, as you shall heare. When it is come to that, that all is ascended, and nothing stayd behind: and the feces are reserved for a further use, as you shal hear hereafter.

CHAP. 16.

THe second reason: the body and spirit must be made indivisible, and be one; for no grosse thing mingleth with the spirit, unlesse the grosse matter bee reduced to a subtility; as into Argent vive; then the one embraceth the other inseparably. For if Argent vive perceiveth a thing like to it selfe, then it rejoyceth, and the dissolved body embraceth the spirit, and suffers him not to fly away, and maketh it durable for the fire, and the spirit rejoyceth, because he hath found his fellow: therefore the one must be like the other; and are of one nature.

CHAP.

CHAP. 17.

Of Dissolution, how to make it.

WEE take leave of *Sol* and *Luna*, thinly beaten, very pure, which we put into a good deale of Mercury, which is made pure also: then we put one after the other into Mercury, in a pot, in a heat not too hot, that the Mercury fume not; when wee see that no grosse thing is in it, and is melted or streameth together, then you wrought well: but if there be any feces, or settlement, then you must adde more Mercury to it, and doe as you did formerly: and this is the first signe of dissolution, that all bee streamy.

CHAP. 18.

The Prosecution of this Matter.

WEE take all the matter thus dissolved, and set in *Balneo Mariæ*; continue the fire for a sennight, then let it coole: take the matter, presse it through a cloth, or skin; if all goeth through, then it is well; if not, begin againe in the vessell with more Mercury, so long till it bee dissolved: the dissolution in Summer is better then in Winter, yet it matters not much.

CHAP. 19.

SEparation, is a dividing of a thing into its members; and a separation of the pure from the impure: we take our dissolved matter, and put it into the smal-
ler

ler veffell, which ftands in the cucurbite, fet the A-limbecke upon, well luted, and fet it in afhes; wee make a continued fire for a fennight, one part of the fpirit fublimeth, which wee call the fpirit or water, and is the fubtileft part; the other part which is not yet fubtile, fticketh about the cucurbite, and fome of it is fallen to the bottome, which we call the ayre, and this part we take warme and moyft, and the third part remayning in the inner veffell, is yet a groffer matter, which ftayeth in the bottome; each of thefe parts we put into a veffell apart, but the third matter wee put more Mercury to, and proceed as formerly, and alwayes each referved apart, and thus you muft proceed: in the inner veffell nothing remayneth but a black powder, which we call the black earth, which is the dregs of the mettalls, which are an obftruction, why mettalls cannot bee united with the fpirit; this powder is of no ufe.

CHAP. 20.

Allegation, or proofe.

YOU may, whereas you have feparated the fowre Elements, from the mettalls, or divided them, and what is the fire then, which is one of the fowre Elements alfo?

CHAP. 21.

ANfwer: We fay, that fire and ayre is of one nature, which are come open together, and mixed together, and the one is turned to the other: but it were hard to be underftood, if you fhould not bee inftructed, structed, that the dividing of the Elements is brought to that, that they have their naturall operation, as in the whole, so in the parts.

CHAP. 22.

WEE call that ayre, which remayned in the bigger vessell, because it is more hot then moist, cold, or dry: the same you must understand also of the other Elements: if they be not sought in particular, they cannot properly bee understood, but are left thus.

Hence *Plato* saith, we turned the moyst into a siccity, and the dry thing we made moyst, and turned the body into water and aire.

CHAP. 23.

WEE say, that sublimation is arising from below upward, as wee see the vapors which fall on the ground and in the water, are exhaled againe by the heat of the sun, and the grosse matter lieth still below, as wee have sayd at the changing of the Elements: thus the matter must be subtiliated, which is not subtile enough, all which must bee done through heat and moistnes, namely through fire and water.

CHAP. 24.

Prosecution of the matter.

KNow that we must take the thing, which remained in the greater vessell, and put the same to other fresh Mercury, that it be well dissolved and subtilized; then we set it in *Balneum Mariæ* for three dais, as formerly: but we mention not the quantity of Mercury

cury, only we leave it to your discretion, as much as you have need, that you may make it fusible, and it be cleare like a spirit: and note, that you take not too much of the Mercury, that it be not a sea: then we set it againe into subliming, as you did formerly, doe it so often, till you have brought it all through the Alimbecke, then it is very subtile, and one thing, cleare, pure, and fusible: then we put it againe into the inner vessell; and let it goe once more through the Alimbeck, and see whether any thing be left behind, to the same more Mercury must be added, till it become all one thing, and yeelds no more sediment, and be separated from all its impurity and superfluity.

CHAP. 25.

Declaration.

I Tell you, that we have made out of two, *viz.* of body and spirit, one onely thing, as a spirit, which is light, and the body is heavy, the spirit quickly and easily flyeth upwards; but our worke is, that the body, which was fixed is now become volatile, and riseth upward, the which is against his nature: Thus wee have made a spirit out of the body, and a body out of the spirit, one onely thing.

CHAP. 26.

Of Fixation, and Congealation.

HAving made a spirit out of the body, which is a thing volatile: now is it requisite to be made fix,

holding

holding in the fire: for we turned the spirit into a body, *viz.* we turned the dry into a moystness, and the moystness into a dryness: now we must make it a thing fix'd: and againe to turne the spirit into a body, and that which formerly rose up, to stay below: and thus have we done according to the sayings of Philosophers, reducing each Element into its contrary, then you will finde what you seek after: namely, make the liquid thing dry; and the dry thing to be liquid, out of a fix a volatile, and the volatile to bee fix: and this can be done only through Congelation; therefore we will turne the spirit into a body.

CHAP. 27.

Coagulation, and Fixation.

How is it done? we take a little of the ferment, which is made of our medicince, be it either *Luna* or *Sol.* and take but a little: as if you have 100 ℔. of the medicine, take but 10 ℔. of the ferment, which must be foliated; and this ferment we amalgamize with the matter which you had before prepared, the same we put into a glasse Violl with a long neck, and set it in a pot of ashes: all which being set in the fit place: then to the above said ferment 2 or 3 fingers, of the spirit, which is gone through the Alimbeck, then wee put a good fire to it for three dayes; then the dissolved body findeth its like, then they embrace one another, each keepeth to its like: then the grosse ferment holdeth with the subtile ferment, attracteth the same, will not let it goe, and the dissolved body, which is

now

now subtile, keepeth the spirit, for they are of an equall subtilty, like one to another, are become one thing; and the fire never may separate them; therfore is it requisite through this means to make the one like the other, and thus the firment, a biding place of the subtile body, and the subtile body a staying place for the spirit, that it may not flye away: then we make fire for a sennight, more or less, yet so long till we see that our matter is congealed. The time of this congelation is either prolonged or shortened, according to the vessells or Ovens condition, and of the fires either continuance, or discontinuing.

CHAP. 28.

A further proceeding in this matter.

WHen you see that this matter is coagulated, then put of the abovesayd matter so much to it, that it be two or three fingers high over it, as you know how it must be done, and put the fire to it as you did formerly, till it bee congealed also, and proceed so long in it till all the matter be congealed. And know that Philosophers for the generallity have concealed the Congelation in their books, and none of them (as far as we can finde) have disclosed it, only *Larikalix*, who hath composed it into many Chapters, and produced it in the German tongue, without any alteration, which he revealed unto me without any reservation or deceit.

Chap.

CHAP. 29.

Calcination.

Having treated of Congealation, and Fixation, now we come to the Calcination. We take the known matter, and put it into an Urinall, and set a head upon it, luting it well, set it in the Oven of ashes, make a continued great fire for a sennight, then that which is not fix riseth into the Alimbeck, which wee call *Hermes* his bird, and that which remaines in the bottome of the glasse, is like ashes, or sifted earth, called the Philosophers Earth, out of which they make their foundation, and out of it they make their increase or augmentation, through heat and moystness: this earth is composed of foure Elements, but are not contrary one to another, for their contrariety is changed or reduced to an agreement unto an uniforme nature: then we take the moyst part, reserve it apart to a further use, which afterward must be put to it, as you shall heare. We take this earth or ashes, which is a very fixed thing, and put it into a strong earthen pot, unto which we lute its lid, and set it in a calcining Oven, that the fire may beat on it above and below; and that fire we continue for three dayes, so that the pot is alwayes red hot, we make of a stone a white calx, and the things which are of water and earth-nature, are of fire's nature; for every calx is of a fires nature, which is hot and dry.

CHAP. 30.

Subtiliation of the foure Elements, into the fifth essence.

WEE have spoken of Calcination, in which we have brought things to the highest subtility, namely, to fire's nature: now we must further subtiliate the foure Elements: we take a little quantity of this Calx, *viz.* if we have 100 pounds, we keep no more than the fourth part, the other we set into dissolution, with a good deale of fresh mercury, even as we had done formerly, and so follow from Chapter to Chapter; from time to time, as formerly hath been proceeded in.

CHAP. 31.

Changing Fire into water.

NOw my dearest, that you may change the fix into a volatile thing, that is Fire into Water; know that that which was of fire's nature, is now become the nature of water, and that which was fix is now become volatile, and being made very subtile; then we take 1. p. of this water, and put it to the reserved Calx, and we adde as much of the water unto, that it go over it two or three fingers breadth over the Calx, then we put fire under for three dayes long, thus it congealeth sooner than at first; for Calx is hot and dry, and sucks in the humidity greedily; this Congelation must be continued till it be quite congealed:

afterward

concerning the Philosophers Stone.

afterward we calcine it as formerly; being quite calcined, it is called the quintessence, because it is of a more subtile nature than Fire, and because of the transmutation formerly made.

CHAP. 32.

The Philosophers Examples.

ALL this being done, then our medicine is finish'd, and nothing but the ingression is wanting, that the matter may have an ingresse into imperfect mettalls.

Plato, and many other Philosophers, begun this worke againe with dissolving, subliming, or subtiliating, congealing, calcining, as at first, and that medicine which we call a ferment, transmutes Mercury into its nature, in which it is dissolved and sublimed; Philophers say, our medicine transmutes infinitely imperfect mettals; and say that he which attaineth once to the perfection of it, hath no more need of it, to make any more; but they speake it mystically in their expressions.

CHAP. 33.

How our medicine transmuteth mettalls into
Sol and Luna.

KNowing that our medicine converteth imperfect mettalls into *Sol* and *Luna,* according to the nature and forme of the matter, out of which it is made;
therefore

therefore know, that, wee now, at second time say, that this our medicine is of that nature, that it transmuteth, converts, divideth asunder like fire, and is of a more subtile nature than fire, for it is of a nature of the quintessences, as we sayd before, therefore it converts Mercury into its nature, seeing our medicine is of a converting nature, as our body converts Mercury into its nature, which is an imperfect body or mettall, and the grossenesse of mettall it turneth into ashes or powder; therefore our medicine is of a dividing, separating nature, as you see fire doth not turn all the world into its nature, but only that which is of its nature, and the rest it turneth to ashes.

CHAP. 34.

Reason why a Spirit is made of a Body.

WEE shewed by reall reason, how a body is turned into a spirit, and againe a spirit is turned into a body, viz. out of a fixed this is made a volatile, and of a volatile a fixed thing; the earth is turned to water and aire, and the aire into fire, and the fire to an earth, the earth into a fire, and the fire is turned to aire, and the aire is turned into water, and the water is become an earth. Now the earth which was of fire's nature, is brought to the nature of quintessence. Thus we have spoken of all the wayes of transmuting, perform'd through heat and moystnesse, and have made out of dry, a moyst thing, and out of the moyst a dry one; otherwise natures, which are of severall motions, and of severall mansions, could not be brought
to

concerning the Philosophers Stone.

to one uniforme thing, if one should bee turned in the others nature.

CHAP. 35.

Accomplishment of Philosophers sayings.

WEE having brought the matter to the above-sayd points, then have we done, and wrought according to the Philosophers sayings, when they say in their Books: Rising from the Earth into Heaven, and comming downe from Heaven into the Earth; to that sense, to make the body which is of earth, into a spirit, which is a subtile thing in his nature, and then to reduce the spirit into a body, which is a grosse low thing, changing one Element into another, as earth into water, water into ayre, ayre into fire; then fire is turned into water, and water into fire, and that into a more subtile nature, and quintessence. Having thus done, then are you come to the glory of the world: be dutifull to God, remember the poore.

CHAP. 36. *Ingression.*

TAke quicke Sulphur, melt it in an earthen vessell, well glazed, being melted, powr it forth into a Lie made of Calx vive, and willow ashes: let all these boyle in a kettle gently, an oyle swimmeth on the top, which take and keepe; having enough of it, we mingle it with sand; distill it through the Alimbeck, so long till it become incombustible: with this oyle wee imbibe our medicine, which will bee like soap, then wee distill by the Alimbeck, and receive the fumes which

which come over, and put it on againe three or foure times, if it hath not enough, then put more of this Oyle to it, being thus imbibed, then put fire under, that the humors may come away, and the medicine be firme and fusible on the body of the glasse. Then we take *Avis Hermetis*, which we reserv'd formerly, and put it to it by degrees, till all be made fix.

CHAP. 37.

Laus Deo.

ACcording to *Avicen*, it is impossible to convert mettals, unlesse they be reduced to their first matter. But by Arts help they are converted into other mettall: we know, that Artists do like Physitians, purging first the corrupted matter, which is obstructive to mans health, then Cordials are ministred, which restore health: so good Artists must proceed in like manner by converting of mettals: first Mercury and Sulphur in metals are purged, whereby they strengthen the heavenly elementall parts in them, according to their desired preparation of metals: then nature worketh further and not Art, but instrumentally helpeth, and then is seen that she really maketh *Sol* and *Luna*. For as the heavenly elementall vertues worke in naturall vessels, even so do the Artificiall, being made uniforme; and as nature worketh through the heat of fire and stars, the same Art effecteth by fire, if temperate and not excessive, for the moving vertue in the matter; for the heavenly vertue in it, mingled at first, inclinable to this or that, is furthered by Art; heavenly

concerning the Philosophers Stone.

venly vertues are communicative to their subjects, as is seen in naturall created things, chiefly in things generated by putrefaction, where the astrall influences are apparent, according to the matters capacity. Artists do imitate herein, destroying one forme to beget another; and his proceedings are best, when they are according unto nature: as by purging the Sulphur by digesting, subliming, and purging Mercury vive; by an exact mixture with the mettals matter, and thus out of their vertues every mettals forme is produced.

The vertue of the converting Element must be predominant, and the parts of it must appeare in the Element converted: and being thus mingled with the Elementated thing, then that Element will have that matter, which made it an Element, and hath the vertue of the other vert. Element. This is that great mystery in this Art.

Scito quod ejus principium est, sicut finis.

The names of the Philosophers Stone, Collected by WILLIAM GRATACOLL.

GOld, Sol, Sun, Brasse of Philosophers, the body of Magnesia, a pure body, clean, ferment of Elixir, Masculine, Argent vive fixt, Sulphur incombustible, Sulphur red, fixed, the rubine stone, kybrik, a man, greene vitrioll, burnt brasse, red earth: the water that is distilled from
these

these things, is named of the Philosophers, the taile of the Dragon, a pure wind, ayre, life, lightning, the house, the afternoone light, virgins milke, sal armoniack, sal niter, the wind of the belly, white fume, red water of sulphur, tartar, saffron, water, the white compound, stinking water, the filthinesse of the dead bloud, Argent vive, a Cucurbite with his Alimbeck, the vessell of the Philosophers, a high man with a Sallet, the belly of a man in the midst, but in the end it is called the foot, or the feet, or on the which feet, or earth is calcined, rosted, congealed, distilled, or made still and quiet, the shaddow of the Sun, a dead body, a crowne overcomming a cloud, the bark of the Sea, Magnesia, black, a Dragon which eateth his tayle, the dregs of the belly, earth found on the dunghill putrified, or in horse dung, or in soft fire, Sulphur, Mercury, secondly in number, and one in essence, name, in name, a stone, body, spirit, and soule; it is called earth, fire, aire, all things, because he containes in him foure Elements; it is called a man or beast, that hath soule, life, body, and spirit, and yet some Philosophers do not thinke the matter to have a soule.

But as it is a stone, it is called the water of Sulphur, the water of the world, the spittle of Lune, the shaddow of the Sun, a donne, Sol, Elephas, white Jayre, eyes of fishes, Beyie, Sulphur, vine sharpe, water, milke, vineger of life, tears, joyning water, Urine, the light of lights, a marvelous Father, Father of Minerals, a fruitfull tree, a living spirit, a fugitive servant, certore of the earth, venome, most strong vineger, white gumme, everlasting water, a woman, a feminine,

nine, a thing of vile price, Azor, menstruous, Brazill, in nature Azot, water, the first matter, the beginning of the world; and mark this, that Argent vive, Mercury, Azot, the full moone, Hypostasis, white lead, or red, do all of them signifie but one thing, our stone, our brasse, our water, Iron, Silver, Lime, whitenesse, Jupiter, Vermilion white, after divers times and degrees of operation.

And note, that the Philosophers washing is to bring againe the whole soule into his body, wherefore you may not understand thereby, the common white washing is convenient to be done with vineger, and salt, and such like.

Also note, that when blackness doth appeare, then it is called dispensation of the man and woman between them, and that the body hath gotten a spirit, which is the tears of the vertues of the soule upon the body, and the body doth revive the action of the soule and spirit, and is made an Eagle and the meane of natures.

And note, that white earth, white Sulphur, white fume, Auripigmentum Magnesia, and Ethell, do signifie all one thing.

Also the stone is called Chaos, a Dragon, a Serpent, a Toad, the green Lion, the quintessence, our stone Lunare, Camelion, most wild black, blacker than black, Virgins milke, radicall humidity, unctuous moysture, liquor, seminall, Salarmoniack, our Sulphur, Naptha, a soule, a Basilisk, Adder, Secundine, Bloud, Spearne, Metteline, haire, urine, poyson, water of wise men, minerall water, Antimony, stinking menstrues, Lead of Philosophers, Sal, Mercury, our
Gold,

Gold, Lune, a bird, our ghost, dun Salt, Alome of Spaine, attrament, dew of heavenly grace, the stinking spirit, Borax, Mercury corporall, wine, dry water, water metelline, an Egge, old water, perminent, *Hermes* bird, the lesse world, Campher, water of life, Auripigment, a body cynaper, and almost with other infinite names of pleasure.

The Secret of Secrets, and Stone of Philosophers.

IF thou desirest to bee so lucky, as that thou mayest obtaine the blessing of Philosophers, as God doth live for ever, so let this verity live with thee.

The Philosophers do very properly say, it tarrieth in the shell, and containeth in himselfe both white and red, the one is called masculine, the other feminine, Animall, Vegetable, and Minerall; there is no such other thing found in this world, that hath both power active, and passive in it, and also hath within him a substance, dead, and quick, spirit and soule, which to the ignorant, the Philosophers do call it the most vile thing, it holdeth in him the foure Elements, contained in his skirts where he is found, and commonly of all men, it may be bought for a small price, it doth ascend by it selfe, he waxeth black, he descendeth and waxeth white, increaseth and decreaseth by himselfe.

It is a matter which the earth bringeth forth, and descends from heaven, waxeth pale and red, is born, is dead, riseth againe, and after liveth for ever; by many wayes it comes to his end, but his proper decoction is upon a fire, soft, meane, strong, it is augmented untill they be sure it resteth quietly with red in the fire;

this

this is according to the vow of all good Philosophers, (called the Philosophers Stone) read and read againe, and every thing more cleare thou shalt never find, and if hereby thou understandest not the matter, thou shalt never otherwise know it, or learne this Art.

Hermes saith, the Dragon is not dead, but with his Brother, and his sister, not by one, but by both together: note these things, three heads and one body, one nature, and one Minerall; and this is sufficient for them which have any aptnesse of understanding in this Science: the Dragon is not mortified nor made fixed, but with *Sol* and *Luna*, and by none other, as saith *Hortulanus* by mountaines in bodies, in the plaine of Mercury, and in these looke for it, and this water is created, and by concourse of these two, is called water permanent of Philosophers.

Our sublimation is to seeth the bodies with golden water, to dissolve, to liquefie, and to sublime them; Our calcination is to putrifie and digest by foure days, and to do no other wayes, wherefore many be deceived in sublimation.

Thou mayest know that brasse which is the Philosophers Gold, is their Gold, and that is true, but thou hast searched for greennesse, thinking that brasse is a Leprous body, which he hath for his greennesse, wherefore I say unto thee, that all that is perfect in brasse, is that greennesse only that is in him, because that that greennesse (by our mastry) is turned shortly into gold, and of this thing we have experience, and if thou wilt prove it we will give thee a rule.

Take therefore burnt brasse, and perfectly rubified, and breake and imboyle him with drinke seaven times,

times, as much as he is able to drinke in all the wayes, of rubifying and roasting him againe, afterward make him to discend, and his greene colour will be made red, as cleare graynes, and thou mayst know that so much redness wil descend with him, that it wil tinckt Argent vive in some part with the very colour of gold, and all this we approved, for it doth worke very great operations; yet thou canst not prepare the Stone by any meanes with any drinke greene and moist, which is seene to be borne in our Minerals. O blessed greatnesse! which doth ingender all things, whereby thou mayst be informed that no vegetable or fruit in budding will appeare, except there be a greene colour; wherefore Philosophers call it their bud, and likewise they call it the water of purifying or putrifaction, and they say the truth heerin; for with his water he is purified & washed from his blackness, and made white, and afterwards he is so made red, whereby thou mayst learne to know that no true tincture is made, but of our brasse; seeth him therefore with his soule, till the spirit be joyned with his body, and be made one, and thou shalt have thy desire. Wise men have spoken of this in many names, but know thou right well, that it is but one matter which doth sticke unto Argent vive, and to bodies, and thou shalt have the true signes; yet left thou shouldest be deceived heereby thou mayst know what Argent vive is to stick unto: Argent vive doth stick to the bodies, which is false; for they think that they do understand that Chapter of *Geber*, of Argent vive, wherein he saith, when in searching in other things, he doth not find by our invention any matter to be more agreeable unto nature then Argent vive

of

of the bodies; for this place is to be underſtood of Argent vive Philoſophicall, for that Argent vive only ſticketh and tarrieth in, and with the bodies: and the old Philoſophers could find no other matter, nor can thoſe which be Philoſophers now invent any other matter which will abide with the bodies, but Argent vive of the Philoſophers; for common Argent vive doth not ſtick to the bodies, but the bodies do ſtick to that Argent vive, and this is certaine by experience; for if the Argent vive common be joyned with any bodies, the Argent vive abides in his proper nature, or flies away, and doth not turne the body into his proper nature, and therefore he doth not cleave unto the bodies; and for this cauſe many be deceived in working in common Argent vive, for our Stone, that is to ſay, Argent vive accidentall which doth advance himſelfe far above Gold, and doth overcome it, and he doth kill, and he doth quicken; for thou muſt know that Argent vive, father of all marvellous things of this our maſtery is congealed, and is both ſpirit and body; and this is that Argent vive which *Gebar* did ſpeake of, the conſideration of a very matter which doth make perfect, is the conſideration of a choſen pure ſubſtance of Argent vive, but chiefly out of whom the ſubſtance of Argent vive may be drawne out is to be inquired of: and we making anſwer do ſay, that in them in whom it is, out of them it may be drawne; therefore Sonne, conſider well, and ſee from whence that ſubſtance is, and take that and none other: if thou deſire to come to knowledge I ſay unto thee, for love of Chriſt that by no other meanes we can it finde; now the Philoſophers never might finde any other matter that would

continue

continue in the fire, but that only which is unctuous, perfect, and incombustible, and that matter, when it is prepared as it ought, will turne all bodes Minerall which it toucheth rightly unto most perfect Sol compleat and above all bodies Lune.

Seeth first with wind, and afterwards without winde, untill thou hast drawne out of thy subject or matter the venome (which is called the soule;) that is it which thou seekest, called the everlasting *aqua-vitæ* for all diseases, the whole mastery is in the vapor. *Avicen.*

Let the body be put in a fire kindled for forty dayes by elementall heat; then in that decoction of forty dayes, the body will rejoyce with the soule, and the soule will rejoyce with the body and spirit, and the spirit will rejoyce with the body and soule, and they are made immortall and perpetuall without separation.

FINIS.

**Teaching Materials
included**

Scan this code to get
your Video Course included in the book, an introduction to the world
of the occult and the paranormal

Or follow this link:

https://templumdianae.co/the-witchy-course/

This Material will give you access to Exclusive training materials to improve in your path !

All rights reserved. No part of this book may be reproduced in any form without the written permission of the copyright owners. All images in this book have been reproduced with the knowledge and prior consent of the artists concerned, and the producer, publisher, or printer accepts no responsibility for any infringement of copyright or otherwise, arising from the contents of this publication. Every effort has been made to ensure that the credits accurately conform to the information provided. We apologize for any inaccuracies and will correct inaccurate or missing information in a subsequent reprint of the book.

Text © 2023 Templum Dianae Media

Printed in the USA
CPSIA information can be obtained
at www.ICGtesting.com
CBHW070449030724
11008CB00017B/965